MARCO PANTANI

THE LEGEND OF A TRAGIC CHAMPION

BOULDER, COLORADO

Marco Pantani: The Legend of a Tragic Champion
© 2005 VeloPress

Printed in the United States of America.

10 9 8 7 6 5 4 3 2 1

Distributed in the United States and Canada by Publishers Group West.

International Standard Book Number: 1-931382-65-4

Library of Congress Cataloging-in-Publication Data

Marco Pantani : the legend of a tragic champion / edited by John Wilcockson.
        p. cm.
   Includes index.
   ISBN 1-931382-65-4 (paperback : alk. paper)
   1. Pantani, Marco. 2. Cyclists—Italy—Biography.
   GV1051.P36M37 2005
   796.6'092—dc22

                                     2005000918

VeloPress
1830 North 55th Street
Boulder, Colorado 80301–2700 USA
303/440-0601 • Fax 303/444-6788 • E-mail velopress@insideinc.com

To purchase additional copies of this book or other VeloPress® books, call 800/234-8356 or visit us on the Web at velopress.com.

Design and composition by Erin Johnson Design

COVER PHOTOS
Pantani at the 1999 Giro d'Italia, stage 19, by Graham Watson; Inset photo of Pantani, taken in the spring of 1993, by Roberto Bettini.

INTERIOR PHOTOS
All interior photos are by Graham Watson, with the following exceptions:
      Childhood, family, and early race photography of Pantani, courtesy of Roberto
          Bettini (pages 8, 14, 16, 18, 20); photo of Pantani in spring of 1993 (second
          photospread, page h).
      1995 world's, Pantani and Induráin (page 43), Conti and Pantani (page 57), 1998
          Tour de France, photos by AFP.

CONTENTS

ACKNOWLEDGMENTS

THIS BOOK IS THE RESULT OF COLLABORATION between the editors of *VeloNews* and some of the European writers who knew Marco Pantani the best. In particular, I would like to thank Pier Bergonzi, chief sportswriter of the Italian newspaper *La Gazzetta dello Sport*, for Chapters 1, 2, 4, 8, 10, 13, 16 and 17. Other writers who have contributed to this work include Sergio Neri of the Italian magazine, *Bicisport* (Chapter 7); Guillaume Prébois of the French monthly, *Vélo Magazine* (Chapter 14); and Michel Beuret of the Swiss weekly, *L'Hebdo* (who conducted the interview with Christina Jonsson in the Epilogue). Parts of other chapters come from *VeloNews* writers Rupert Guinness (Chapter 5) and Charles Pelkey (Chapter 11). In keeping with the voice of the original author, some chapters retain present tense verbs. Mark Deterline performed the Italian translations, with passion and perfectionism. Graham Watson took the majority of the photographs in this book. Also, many thanks to Amy Rinehart for seeing the possibilities of this title, and to Renee Jardine of VeloPress for managing a complicated project with energy and efficacy.

John Wilcockson

MOLTI RAGAZZI HANNO PERSO LA SPERANZA DELLA GIUSTIZIA

Sono stato umiliato per nulla. Per quattro anni sono in tutti i tribunali, ho solo perso la mia voglia di essere come tanti altri sportivi, ma il ciclismo ha pagato e molti ragazzi hanno perso la speranza della giustizia. E io mi sto ferendo con la deposizione di una verità sul mio documento, perchè il mondo si renda conto che se tutti i miei colleghi hanno subìto umiliazioni, in camera con le telecamere nascoste per cercare di rovinare le famiglie, e poi dopo come fai a non farti male. Io non so come mai mi fermo in casi di sfogo come questi. Mi piacerebbe, io so di aver sbagliato con le prove però, ma solo quando la mia vita sportiva, soprattutto privata, è stata violata ho perso molto. E sono in questo paese con la voglia di dire che hasta la victoria *è un grande scopo per uno sportivo.*

Ma il più difficile è di aver dato il cuore per uno sport, con incidenti e infortuni: e sempre sono ripartito. Ma cosa resta, c'è tanta tristezza e rabbia per le voilenze che la giustizia a tempi è caduta nel credere. Ma la mia storia spero che sia di esempio agli altri sport che le regole, sì, ma devono essere uguali per tutti. Non esiste lavoro che per esercitare si deve dare il sangue, i controlli di notte alle famiglie degli atleti. Io non mi sono sentito più sereno di non essere controllato in casa, in albergo, dalle telecamere e sono finito per farmi del male, per non rinunciare alla mia intimità, all'intimità della mia donna, e degli altri colleghi che hanno perso. E molte storie di famiglie violentate. Ma andate a vedere cos' è un ciclista e quanti uomini vanno in mezzo alla torrida tristezza per cercare di ritornare con quei sogni di uomo che si infrangono con le droghe: ma dopo la mia vita di sportivo. E se un pò di umanità farà capire e chiedere cosa ci fa sperare e che con uno sbaglio vero si capisce e si batte, perchè si sta dando il cuore. Questo documento è verità, la mia speranza è che un uomo vero o una donna legga e si ponga in difesa di chi, come si deve dire al mondo, regole per sportivi uguali per tutti. E non sono un falso, mi sento ferito e tutti i ragazzi che mi credevano devono parlare.

Ciao Marco.

[Translator's note: The English version of Marco Pantani's "last letter" is a translation that strives to be true to Marco's original text. This means that the English translation reads the same way Marco's own words read. It has not been corrected for grammar, which would have resulted in a less authentic rendition. —Mark Deterline]

A LOT OF PEOPLE HAVE LOST THEIR FAITH IN JUSTICE

I was humiliated for nothing. For four years I was in all the courts, but all I lost was my desire to be like lots of other athletes. It's cycling that has paid the price, and a lot of people have lost their faith in justice. I am hurting myself with this deposition of truth in my passport, so that the world will realize that if all of my colleagues have suffered humiliations, in rooms with hidden television cameras in an attempt to ruin families; how, then, do you avoid getting hurt as a result? I don't know why I stop myself in moments of venting like this. I would like, I know I failed the tests but, however only when my life as an athlete, especially my personal life, was violated, I lost so much. And I'm in this country with the desire to say that *hasta la victoria* has great significance for an athlete.

But the hardest thing is to have given my heart for a sport, with accidents and misfortune: and I always came back. But what's left, there is so much sadness and anger as a result of the injustices that the legal system at times allowed itself to believe in. But I hope that my story will serve as an example to other sports; rules, yes, but they should be the same for everyone. There is no other type of work that requires you to give blood to perform it, nighttime tests in the family homes of athletes. I didn't feel any more at peace by not being tested at home, in a hotel, in front of television cameras and I ended up hurting myself, in order not to give up my privacy, my girlfriend's privacy, and that of other colleagues who have suffered. And many stories of violated families. But go and see what a cyclist is and how many men are passing through the depths of sadness in an attempt to come back with dreams of men that are shattered by drugs: but after my athletic career. And if a little humanity will help people understand and ask what will give us hope and that a real mistake makes you understand and fight, because you're giving your heart. This document is truth, my hope is that a real man or woman will read it and will take a stand in defense of those, like we need to say to the world, rules for athletes that apply equally to everyone. And I'm not a fake, I feel injured and all those who believed me must speak.

Ciao, Marco.

Worshipped, Abused, Rejected

HE LIVED THE FRENETIC LIFE of a celebrated sports icon. He died the solitary death of a drug-dependent depressive.

Marco Pantani's ending faithfully reflected his star-crossed life and times. The quirky, pugnacious Italian climber was frequently alone at the end of punishing mountain stages in cycling's greatest races, minutes ahead of the opposition. And he was alone again, tragically so, when he died in the fifth-story room of a hotel called Le Rose in the afternoon of a somber St. Valentine's Day in February 2004. Outside his window, life still bustled in the streets of Rimini, while waves continued to foam onto the beach of this Adriatic resort.

Pantani was 34.

On February 18, some 20,000 people came to Pantani's hometown of Cesenatico, fewer than 20 kilometers north of Rimini. They watched and applauded his final 2-kilometer journey: from his funeral at the church of San Giacomo, where he was baptized, then alongside the Leonardo da Vinci–designed port canal, to his burial at the small coastal town's cemetery.

His grave has become a shrine, like that of Italy's other tragic cycling champion who died before his time, Fausto Coppi, who was just 40 and still an active racer when he was claimed by malaria that had been misdiagnosed as the flu.

Twenty thousand Il Pirata *fans came to Marco Pantani's funeral on February 18, 2004.*

Like Coppi, Pantani was revered for the transcendent manner in which he raced his celeste-green Bianchi bicycle to victories at the Giro d'Italia and Tour de France. But unlike Coppi, whose exploits straddled World War II and were followed by pockets of fans huddled around crackly radios, Pantani was an electrifying presence to live television audiences of hundreds of millions of people.

As a consequence, fame was thrust on Pantani at a rate and in a manner that he had a hard time handling. Outwardly, he promulgated his notoriety by shaving his head, growing a goatee, piercing his ears for small silver hoop earrings, and wearing a knotted bandanna that bore the skull-and-crossbones emblem of *Il Pirata*, The Pirate.

But inwardly, Pantani was perplexed. At press conferences, he often talked of himself in the third person, as if the public Pantani were someone else. But when the swashbuckling image of "the little guy who could" was shattered by

Eight months before his death, Pantani placed 14th at the 2003 Giro d'Italia.

his blood hematocrit testing above cycling's legal limit on the eve of a second Giro triumph in 1999, Pantani was crushed.

Ridiculed by those quick to jump to conclusions, humiliated in the press by accusations of doping, and subsequently hounded by no less than seven judicial inquiries into alleged crimes of "sporting fraud," Pantani became more and more depressed.

The bicycle was his only true antidote to the personal onslaught. He rode it joyfully through the hills of Romagna to the southwest of his home-town. He later raced it to a pair of mountaintop stage wins ahead of Lance Armstrong at the 2000 Tour. And he came back again in the last summer of his life to show vestiges of his fiery climbing style in a 14th-place finish at the Giro. But for most of the final four and a half years, Pantani was chained to a nighttime world of discos, disillusion, and drugs.

He still had the trappings of success, but the troubled champion crashed his fast cars, abandoned his gated mansion, and in the early summer of 2003 split with his longtime Danish girlfriend, Christina Jonsson. After last-minute plans failed in June 2003 to get him a Tour de France ride on Jan Ullrich's Bianchi team, Pantani was shattered.

He checked into the Parco dei Tigli, a high-class Padua clinic specializ-ing in the treatment of nervous disorders. His personal manager and friend, Manuela Ronchi, said at the time, "I don't know anything. I can only say that he must be suffering with something very private and that he doesn't want to talk about it to anyone."

His condition, which may have been incorrectly diagnosed, was treated with antidepressants. On leaving the clinic, he didn't return to the bike. He became bloated: as much as 50 pounds over the sleek 125-pound climbing machine that took 36 race wins (half of them at the Giro and the Tour) in 12 years of professional cycling.

He was interviewed for the last time in September 2003 by Mario Pugliese, a boyhood friend and writer with the *Voce di Romagna*. He told Pugliese, "The champion I was exists no more; he is far from the man that I have become." Pantani was dismissive of his fans in his last interview. "If they still cheer me, it's not through affection but because they have need of a personality." And he was tired of being that personality, Pugliese wrote.

Four months later, a 34th birthday party was thrown for Pantani by a friend, a disco owner. A dozen people came to this last supper. Recalling that evening, Pugliese told French journalist Philippe Brunel, "In the middle of the meal, Marco stood up, took from his pocket a packet of cocaine in front of everyone. He went to the toilets, followed by a friend who wanted to stop him. The two argued. The evening degenerated. On leaving, all his friends said to themselves, 'This is the last time that we'll see him.' Marco had arrived at the ultimate stage of dependence."

The day after his death, Pantani was honored by schoolchildren at the Tour of Liguria bike race.

Pantani still had hopes of kicking his drug habit. He twice visited Cuba, where a friend, the ex–Argentinean soccer star Diego Maradona, had been treated for cocaine addiction. On February 27, Pantani was due to fly to Bolivia with a priest who runs a secluded detoxification center for young people.

But 13 days before departure, and five days after checking into Le Rose hotel in Rimini, Pantani's heart failed. An autopsy pointed to fluid on the brain and in the lungs as contributors to his death. The final verdict was cocaine poisoning. Like rock stars Jimi Hendrix, Janis Joplin, and Jim Morrison, it seemed that Pantani's bright star had burned out on a diet of drugs.

On nine pages of his passport, which was found next to his bed at the Rimini hotel, Pantani wrote: "I'm left all alone. No one managed to understand me. Even the cycling world and even my own family." Also included were some loving words for his estranged girlfriend, who must have been on his mind that Valentine's Day. He then addressed his dependence on drugs. "I want to go to Bolivia to break this addiction," he wrote. "I want to finish with that world, and I want to get back on the bike."

Tragically, this was one uphill battle that not even Marco Pantani could conquer.

He Drank Life
in Large Gulps

No, HE WASN'T ABLE TO BE THE LEAST BIT ORDINARY. He was never ordinary. The life of Marco Pantani, the kid from Cesenatico, on the Adriatic coast of Italy, is a long and twisted account of strange events—a collection of stories about pushing limits. He was the kind of kid who drove at night with the headlights off, the first in his peer group to get his ear pierced, the first to get a tattoo, the first to grow a soul patch, and the first to go over 200 kilometers per hour (125 mph) on a Harley or in a Jaguar. The first . . . Marco couldn't accept being second to anyone, not even at pinball.

But he was also a man pushing the limits of sweetness and shyness. He was so fragile that in the end he wasn't able to handle the weight of the lingering questions. Those who tried to get inside his head—and there were many—came away with wonderful revelations. Few, however, understood the internal conflicts of the kid who just wanted to ride a bicycle over the mountains.

Marco never did anything in half measures. Thinning hair? Away with it, better shaved off. A couple of pounds overweight heading into an event? Nothing but popcorn for two days. His fitness test? Eight hours of cycling

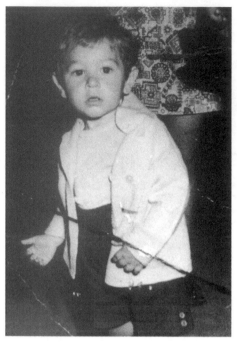

Even as a child, Marco was very independent, a leader.

with nothing but a slice of watermelon for dinner to see how his body would handle it.

In the mountains, he would hear voices and attack, again and again, to "shorten the agony." It was as if he were always trying to escape from himself. As if, every time, he had to prove something to somebody. Since his childhood, he had been the classic leader of the gang. He would sneak off to the beach and organize adventures. His dad, Papà Paolo, loved him so much that he looked at his relationship with Marco as a calling. Mamma Tonina is like him, strong and fragile at the same time. From the time he was little, Marco had spent as much time as possible with Grandpa Sotero, a legendary figure in the mind of the young man who would become *Il Pirata*. Sometimes Marco would hear the voice of his grandfather, which accompanied him all his life.

In school, Marco always made it through by virtue of his extraordinarily energetic ingenuity. Studying wasn't his strong suit, but when he needed to qualify for the next grade, he would cram for two weeks and complete his coursework. Then he would concentrate on his favorite ice cream, flatbread wraps, sausages, bowls of *mascarpone* . . . and his closest friends. His gang was always gaining new members and nicknames, but he was always the leader. Pet names were another of Marco's specialties. Papà Paolo was Ferdinando,

Pantani won seven mountaintop stage finishes at the Tour, six at the Giro.

Mamma Tonina was Koni, and his sister Laura was now known by all as Manola. The same was true for Marco's cycling teammates, from Mortadella (Fabiano Fontanelli) to Hubner (Marcello Siboni) to Brontolo (Roberto Conti).

Friends still remember his first car, a Fiat Ritmo hatchback, which finished its adventurous life by slamming into the side of a house. Prior to that, it had survived a rollover in a field; four people were in the car when it happened, and only the driver, Marco, came away without a scratch. Those accidents were the first of a long series of car crashes. Pantani devoured Porsches, Jaguars, and Mercedes-Benzes. He pushed all of his cars to their limit, and sometimes beyond.

A young teenaged Marco got into cycling by chance with the Fausto Coppi School of Cycling in Cesenatico. He found himself with a bike, a jersey, and a pair of cycling shorts. What more could a little kid whose head was filled with dreams want?

Above all, those dreams carried him into the mountains. He was so strong and so sure of himself that his performances bordered on masochism. He looked forward to mountaintop finishes when he would drop back to the rear of the group, then experience the thrill of passing everyone to win—just as he did at the 1999 Giro following his crash on the climb toward Santuario d'Oropa.

Marco drank life in large gulps. At night on the Riviera Romagnola, with its beaches and discotheques along the Adriatic, he never held back. On the contrary, his behavior was often marked by indulgence. Nature had given him extraordinary qualities. He needed only two weeks to get into shape. He needed only two hours of sleep to feel perky.

The public Pantani was larger than life.

However, his life was an obstacle course. There was his crash on May 1, 1995, which cost him that year's Giro, and the head-on collision with a Jeep on the Pino Torinese descent in October 1995, which fractured his tibia and fibula and cost him a whole season. And then there was another crash on the descent of the Chiunzi, which meant good-bye to the 1997 Giro. Between one accident and another, Marco climbed back on the bike and would sometimes test his fitness in a Gran Fondo, a mass-participation long-distance race, riding in a wig to disguise himself.

Pantani had scars all over his body, mixed with tattoos, a little Milanese devil on his shoulder and a butterfly on his chest. An earring and a bandanna always comprised another of his distinguishing get-ups. The earring, especially, was the umpteenth challenge to his father. When Paolo, or rather Ferdinando, first saw it, he said, "There's not room for the two of you here. It's either you or it." In the end, both would stay: Marco and his earring.

To hear his friends tell it, he had often been in love. But there was only one love of his life: Christina Jonsson, the small blonde Dane with whom he had a long, tender, and at the same time tempestuous relationship. It was with her that Pantani enjoyed painting. The end of that relationship is another important part of understanding the nature of the black hole that Marco ended up in. The 45 pounds he put on over the winter when he worked at being a *culturista*, the two trips to Cuba at the outer reaches of the real world, the last quarrels with his parents, and the distance he put between himself and his friends were part of a Pantani who was no longer himself—a man who had become his alter ego.

The Kid from
the Coast

ON CERTAIN DAYS IN THE WINTER, Cesenatico seems like a city of the Great White North. It's so cold that you can feel comfortable only in a small bar with a cappuccino and a pastry. Snowflakes as big as butterflies can appear in the frozen and humid air.

It was on such a day that Marco Pantani, while walking along the port canal, was trying to put together the pieces of his past as a kid from the coast. Now he was king of the mountains, an enigmatic paradox from that wonderful and contradictory region that is Romagna, an enigmatic miracle from that little seaside town that at Christmas seems like a big village, and on August 15, in the middle of the Italian holiday season, seems to grow eight times in size.

A renowned and wealthy champion, Pantani was the manifestation of a complex personality. He was a man with a fierce desire to succeed, but who was also shy in a tender and disarming way. There was something special about him, unique, something that made him a celebrity as well as a champion. Pantani belonged to that category of people who make life an art form. Had he not possessed that curse of a talent on a bike, he could have been a superstar of rock 'n' roll, the arts, or cuisine. He would have brought to any undertaking the quality that money can't buy even over the Internet: charisma.

MARCO IS BORN ON ONE OF THOSE COLD winter days, January 13, 1970, in Bufalini de Cesena, just inland from Cesenatico. His father, Ferdinando, is a plumber. His typical Italian family—father, mother (Tonina), and two children (Laura

Marco's parents, Ferdinando and Tonina (pictured here with their grandchildren), were proud of their son's achievements.

and Marco)—live a dignified life, without luxuries. Papà is often away from home for work, and little Marco spends much of his time with Grandpa Sotero, who teaches him to recognize the subtleties in life and the secrets of the sea.

The family apartment on via dei Mille 3, between Boschetto and the beach, is too small to contain Marco's energy. Though short, shabby, and frail, this boy from Cesenatico is a born leader. He's the leader of the gang in Boschetto. When there's a game or group event to organize, or when there's a fight, Marco is always in the middle of things. School doesn't interest him. He's smart enough to get by, but studies don't figure into his lifestyle.

But sports do interest him, particularly soccer. Agile and quick, he plays on the right flank for Cesenatico. He doesn't tolerate even the thought of sitting on the bench. But the squad is too large and the constant turnover makes it too impersonal. So, as soon as the "gang of troublemakers" offers him an alternative, he doesn't let it pass him by.

The alternative is called the Fausto Coppi School of Cycling. One day Marco is passing by the Bar del Corso, headquarters of the cycling club, and sees that orange soda and pastries are being served. Inside are his wildest friends: Battistini, Balsassare, Agostini, Budini, and Lombardi. Pantani has already ridden with these guys on a training ride toward Savignano. His friends had impeccable bikes, while he, the little guy, had his father's basic one. Marco was wearing himself out, but he didn't give up. In the end, after the customary loop of about 50 kilometers, he was exhausted but happy. Cycling is his sport, he decides.

Pantani enters the Bar del Corso and doesn't need to be convinced; he already knows. Along with a white-and-blue cycling jersey, they lend him a silver Vicini bike, like the ones provided by the Italian Cycling Federation. Papà Paolo and Mamma Tonina need only to buy cycling shoes in place of soccer cleats. Nicola Amaducci, the soul of the Fausto Coppi School, welcomes him

15

At age 14, Marco rode his red Vicini racing bike to his very first victory.

with open arms and puts him with a compelling group of very young boys born in 1970.

Marco is seduced by bike racing, which little by little overshadows all of his other interests. A year later he receives his very own Vicini bicycle as a gift—in bright red. It's Grandpa Sotero's idea. Of the 280,000-lire (roughly $200) price tag, he pays 160,000 of it. Papà Pantani covers the rest. Marco's cycling experience is very different with the new red machine; he will never love another bike as intensely. After every training ride, he takes it into the house to wash it in the bathtub with soap and big sponges.

Soon he's racing with the novices. On April 22, 1984, he has his first win at a race in Case Missiroli near Cesena—a solo breakaway. The ball is rolling; several victories follow in rapid succession in Serravcalle, Pieve di Quinto, and Pieve di Noce.

In 1985, Pantani moves up to the junior category, still with the Fausto Coppi club, but he's now in a group directed by Vittorio Savini, who will one day become president of Marco's major fan club. Savini often recalls the cockiness and lucidity of his pupil. In races with climbs, Marco is commonly found at the back of the group. The *direttore sportivo* yells and complains, but Pantani then passes everyone and wins or is the first over the summit. He does it that way on purpose. He enjoys feeling omnipotent in the mountains. He likes the fact that it is his exclusive domain of conquest. But he does have a challenger who pushes him to the limits of pain and beyond: himself.

Pantani tries to get a diploma. He registers at the Istituto Agrario, then switches to a three-year course in electronics. He postpones the last year of English classes and then doesn't pass the make-up exam. He has only bike racing on his mind.

MARCO JOINS THE RINASCITA RAVENNA cycling squad to race with the amateurs before moving to the Gaicobazzi di Nonantola, the most prestigious under-23 team in Emilia-Romagna. There he finds Giuseppe Roncucci, the trainer Marco will always remember as one who played a decisive role in taking his cycling to the next level. Marco wins the mountain time trials up the Futa Pass and the Piccolo Emilia. In 1990, at age 20, he finishes third at the amateurs' Giro d'Italia behind Wladimir Belli and Ivan Gotti. In the following year's edition, he wins the stage at Agordo and finishes second overall behind Francesco Casagrande. Marco also earns his first azure-blue Italian national team jersey for the Settimana Bergamasca, a race that is won by a certain Lance Armstrong.

Beppe Martinelli, a talent scout for the Carrera pro team, is already on Pantani's trail. In 1992, Marco's graduation to the pros is assured when he finally wins the amateur Giro d'Italia by blowing the race apart in the Dolomites, thanks to stage wins at Cavalese and Alleghe. He returns to Cesenatico the happiest man in the world. But he is told that Grandpa Sotero is in the hospital: He will die the next day, and Marco loses a source of guidance in his emerging life.

Pantani's hair was still thick when he won the amateurs' Giro d'Italia at age 22.

THE DOOR TO THE PRO PELOTON opens on August 5, 1992, at the Gran Premio di Camaiore race. The kid from Cesenatico makes his debut in the Carrera team jersey. He preferred it to other, more lucrative offers because it's a team led by Italian star Claudio Chiappucci and one that enabled Irishman Stephen Roche to take victories at the Giro and Tour de France in 1987. So Carrera has an international flavor and qualifies for the grand tours. Marco debuts with a solid 12th place at Camaiore in a race won by Davide Cassani. A month later, he takes third place at the Gastone Nencini Memorial hill climb. He is adapting well to the new challenge.

Marco starts his first full pro season in 1993. In mid-May, he comes in fifth at the difficult Giro del Trentino and is ready to help his team leader, Chiappucci, challenge the Spaniard Miguel Induráin in his first Giro d'Italia. But Marco develops tendinitis, and he is forced to abandon with four stages left when he finishes 18th in the general classification. Like anyone else in his or her early years, he has to learn by experience.

In 1994 it is a different story. He takes fourth place at the Trentino and then fourth at the Tour of Tuscany. Those performances confirm his steady progress, but in the Giro that follows just afterward, two days in the Dolomites, stages 14 and 15, turn Marco's life upside down and proclaim the birth of a new phenomenon.

The 24-year-old Pantani is supposed to be at Chiappucci's side, but at a certain point he is given the green light by his sports director. Going into the 235-kilometer stage between Lienz in Austria and Merano in the Italian Dolomites, over five mountain passes, Pantani is situated 10th overall more than six minutes behind the race leader, Russia's Evgueni Berzin. Little attention is paid to the small, balding rider on the Carrera team when he takes off

Breakthrough! Pantani beat the best in the 1994 Giro stage over the Mortirolo.

from the main group in search of a breakaway group who has been up the road for most of the long day. Pantani overtakes all but one of the breakaways on the last climb, the Monte Giovo; then on the wet, slick descent, he catches up to and passes the solo leader, Pascal Richard of Switzerland. Pantani wins the stage by 40 seconds over Gianni Bugno and Chiappucci, and moves up to sixth overall. It is Marco's first victory as a professional.

He doesn't have much time to pat himself on the back. The next day, there are another seven hours in the saddle on a wet, cold stage when Giro race director Carmine Castellano's menu includes the legendary Stelvio and Mortirolo passes. For many the 12-kilometer, 10 percent Mortirolo is the mother of all climbs. Pantani attacks right at its base, splitting the race apart. Berzin, in the *maglia rosa*, tries to respond, but falls back. Two-time defending champion Induráin resists with sheer grit. Bugno is dropped. Marco grinds away through the switchbacks and continues his charge. He summits alone and becomes the hero of the Mortirolo, devouring it in 43.53, a whopping 2:07 faster than Franco Chioccioli's hill-climb record of 1991.

Induráin, Belli, Chiappucci, and the Colombian Nelson Rodriguez catch up to Marco on the descent. No problem. On the Santa Cristina, as soon as the route begins to climb again with some 15 percent pitches, Pantani begins to torture his bike again. He opens a gap. At the finish in Aprica he is first, putting 2:52 on Chiappucci and 3:37 on Belli. Induráin arrives 3:30 behind, Berzin at 4:06, and Bugno and Pavel Tonkov at 5:50. Marco climbs to second place overall, on the heels of Berzin, another kid born in 1970. "On the summits, I could feel the breath of the fans, I could feel my hair stand on end," Pantani says.

"Pantani, you're a legend," reads the headline on the front page of the *Gazzetta dello Sport*, paraphrasing the smash hit of the Italian pop group 883. The legend of Marco Pantani is indeed born on the Mortirolo, the mountain that would await his arrival in pink in 1999, but then never see him again. At the end of the 1994 Giro, he is second, one step on the podium lower than Berzin and one above Induráin. Riding the wave of enthusiasm, the kid from Cesenatico goes to the Tour de France "to make life hard for Miguel."

The tall rider from Navarre is a man of few words but of great pride, and he has yet to swallow his Aprica defeat. That kid who attacked right in front of him on the Mortirolo and then on the Santa Cristina needs to be taught a lesson. At this time, Induráin is the king of the Tour, an enlightened monarch. All he has to do is win the time trials and then keep his adversaries in check in the mountains. He systematically leaves the stage wins to his "friends." Like the day at Hautacam: on the mountain that rises above Lourdes, Pantani is the strongest, but Induráin clears the way for a Frenchman, Luc Leblanc, to win the stage. The Pirate finishes only third, 18 seconds back.

In the Alps, Marco could have won at Val Thorens, but he crashes on a flat section of the Glandon climb and bangs his right knee. For a few very long moments, there is fear he will abandon. Injured and angry, Marco climbs back on his bike and catches up to the small group of leaders. He again drops Induráin, but he's not able to catch up to Rodriguez and Piotr Ugrumov, who had already broken away. Again, he finishes third, as he does on the podium on the Champs-Élysées in Paris, behind Induráin and Ugrumov.

SECOND AT THE GIRO AND THIRD at the Tour, Italy has a new man for the stage races. National coach Alfredo Martini recruits Pantani onto the Italian team for the world championships in Agrigento, but as an alternate—a big disappointment for someone who has always hated sitting on the bench.

Pantani spends the winter of 1994–1995 cultivating his dreams, focusing above all on the Giro. But destiny sees otherwise. On May 1, at a road intersection in Santarcangelo di Romagna, he has an encounter with a small Fiat. The accident signals a good-bye to the "race of pink." Marco swallows the setback, then shows up for the Tour of Switzerland, where he wins the toughest mountain stage, which finishes at the top of the Flumserberg. He goes to the Tour de France extremely determined, but the time trials and an imperious Induráin don't allow him opportunities to wear the yellow jersey. Marco concentrates on winning major stages in the mountains. And he leaves his mark.

He wins at L'Alpe d'Huez, taking back almost a minute and a half on Induráin and Swiss star Alex Zülle. A stage in the Pyrenees, finishing at Guzet Neige, provides him with another mountaintop victory. The next day, on the Portet d'Aspet descent, Fabio Casartelli, also born in 1970, is killed. Pantani, who was his friend, is among the most devastated.

Martini again offers Marco an "azure" Italian National Team jersey, and this time Marco is one of the captains for the world championships in Colombia. The course at Duitama is made for climbers. But it rains. Pantani has the strength to drop everyone, but his wheels are slipping and he can't get out of the saddle. It is good for the two big motors, Spaniards Abraham Olano and Induráin. Miguel is the most closely watched. Olano takes advantage of that and wins solo. Then Induráin beats Pantani and Mauro Gianetti in the sprint for second place. Marco steps onto the podium to accept the bronze medal with a grim look. He knows that a big opportunity has passed him by.

He returns to Italy convinced that he can also be a contender at the season-ending Tour of Lombardy classic, but he ends up watching the "Race of the Falling Leaves" on TV at a hospital in Turin. During the final kilometers of the Milan-Turin race, Pantani is struck by a Jeep on the descent from Pino Torinese. The impact is violent, and the prognosis devastating: Both his tibia and fibula have multiple fractures. The entire 1996 season is already a wash.

Months of rehabilitation followed Pantani's devastating crash at Milan-Turin in October 1995.

THE FOLLOWING SUMMER, WHILE STILL getting around on crutches, Marco wins the confidence of Romano Cenni, Mr. Mercatone Uno, the owner of one of Italy's largest supermarket chains. The two like and understand each other, and Cenni creates a pro cycling team that will assist Marco in becoming *Il Pirata*. The nickname is suggested by his journalist friend Bruno Sueri, editor of *Ciclismo Illustrato*.

A woman is now seen regularly at Pantani's side: Christina Jonsson, a blonde Dane with the face of a model. She dances on the raised platforms at discotheques along the Riviera Romagnola, and later studies at the Accademia d'Arte in Ravenna. The Pirate falls for her and asks if she would be interested in working at his parents' flatbread stand in Cesenatico. Of his various romances, the one with Christina is the love of Marco's life.

A new season gets under way—it's now 1997—and Marco's primary objective is the same as always: the Giro's *maglia rosa*. He shows up at the start in Venice convinced that he has the legs and head to blow the race apart. But he forgets that uncomfortable companion that is his destiny. This time (again) it takes the form of a black cat that runs out in front of him on the descent at Chiunzi on the Amalfi coast. Picking himself up from the crash, he somehow gets to the finish of this eighth stage, but spends that evening at the hospital in Cava dei Tirreni. The next day, he's back home.

Again, the Tour de France becomes the soil in which his comeback blossoms. It's the year of Jan Ullrich, who appears to be the new Induráin. Extremely good at time trialing and excellent in the mountains, the imposing German appears to be inaugurating a new reign. Pantani takes great satisfaction in putting the hurt on "the Kaiser," flying up to L'Alpe d'Huez in record time. He does an encore performance at Morzine two days later, after a brilliant climbing solo on the Joux-Plane. In Paris, he's again on the podium, third behind Ullrich and Richard Virenque.

Over the winter, The Pirate's determination becomes even stronger. Mercatone Uno prepares itself to face the "season of seasons." Mercatone Uno's team director, Luciano Pezzi, decides to take the group on a retreat in Terracina, on the coast between Rome and Naples, where he went with the last Italian Tour champion, Felice Gimondi, in the 1960s. It is a good decision. Pantani starts the season by winning the most demanding stage of the Tour of

Defending champion Pavel Tonkov (right) just wasn't strong enough to hang on to Pantani as he attacked on the Montecampione climb at the 1998 Giro.

Murcia in Spain. He attacks on the Morron de Totana climb and then beats Alberto Elli and Alex Vinokourov. From then on, it's a long list of victories. At the Giro, *Il Pirata* initially leaves the big horse Zülle some breathing room, but wins at the high-elevation finish in Pampeago and takes flight in the Dolomites. He attacks with Giuseppe Guerini on the Marmolada, leaving the stage to his breakaway companion in Selva di Val Gardena. While doing so, he pulls on his first ever *maglia rosa*. This hallowed jersey, bearing the color of the race sponsor, the *Gazzetta dello Sport*, remains his until Milan, thanks also to his winning exploit on the climb to Montecampione, when he hears "a voice" a few kilometers from the finish, casts away the little diamond from his nose piercing, and drops the last of his rivals, Russian Pavel Tonkov, once and for all.

Now that he's won the *maglia rosa*, Marco returns to Cesenatico to enjoy his victory his way. He gives big hugs to Mamma Tonina and his fiancée, Christina, who are waiting for him at the flatbread stand. Then he pretends to go to the bathroom, and escapes (from even the journalists) out the window to spend the night in local discotheques with his friends. He reappears at six o'clock in the morning at the Bar dei Marinai.

But the celebration in June is spoiled by the unexpected death of his mentor, Luciano Pezzi, at age 77. It is a trial for Marco. In tribute to the man who had the most influence on him, Pantani decides to race the Tour, even though he's not in the best of form. In the time-trial prologue at Dublin,

Marco bleached his beard to celebrate victory at the 1998 Tour, where Ullrich (left) and Julich shared the Paris podium.

Ireland, he registers the fifth-to-last time. He seems out of contention and keeps a low profile until the mountains. In the Pyrenees he regains precious time from Ullrich at Luchon, where he finishes second, 36 seconds behind Rodolfo Massi, and above all at Plateau de Beille, where he wins solo. But it's on the Galibier that Marco pulls off a true exploit, perhaps the greatest of his career, to win the Tour. On a hellish day, *Il Pirata* attacks continually until he breaks Ullrich. On the descent of the Galibier, he takes every possible risk and then reels in, one by one, the breakaway riders to win the stage at the finish in Les Deux-Alpes, more than eight minutes ahead of "the Kaiser." The yellow jersey is his.

This is the Tour of the "Festina Affair," of the *soigneur* (trainer) who is stopped at Customs with a car full of drugs. It's the Tour that risked his not making it to Paris. But it's also the Tour of Pantani and of that historic stage in the fog of the Galibier, bearing the mark of The Pirate. Now he is a personality recognized all over the planet. Man of the year in Italian sports, he renews the general public's interest in bike racing.

IN 1999, MARCO GETS off TO ANOTHER flying start. He wins the Aledo stage and the final overall classification at the Murcia race, and takes the stage in Empuria Brava at the Setmana Catalana. At the Giro d'Italia he's the absolute boss. Early on, he leaves Laurent Jalabert some room, only to come on the scene and dominate the show at every finish in the mountains: Gran Sasso, Oropa (with a spectacular comeback after a crash), Pampeago, and Madonna di Campiglio. The only thing left to do is put the dot on the exclamation point in Aprica, after the Gavia and Mortirolo climbs, while wearing the pink jersey. But he's halted by the Union Cycliste Internationale's (UCI) special commission:

His hematocrit level is too high (52 percent, two points higher than permissible), which results in immediate expulsion from the race and 15 days' "rest." The Giro is in shock. His clan speaks of a conspiracy. Paolo Savoldelli, who was in second place, refuses to put on the *maglia rosa*. The stage is won by Spaniard Roberto Heras, the Giro by Italian Ivan Gotti.

Pantani says, "I'll never race again." It's not true, but almost. Marco returns to racing in 2000. He's still able to be a player at the Giro, where he contributes to teammate Stefano Garzelli's victory. At the Tour, he wins the Mont Ventoux stage, in which Armstrong is condescendingly altruistic, as well as the Courchevel stage.

The Giro is in shock. His clan speaks of a conspiracy. Paolo Savoldelli, who was in second place, refuses to put on the *maglia rosa*.

But after June 5, 1999, he's not himself anymore. From that day in Madonna di Campiglio onward, Pantani the athlete begins to die. And not only the athlete.

He's in San Remo when *carabinieri* officers from the Italian narcotics department cause a firestorm at the Giro d'Italia by confiscating a large number of prohibited drugs. Taking all the investigations into consideration, open or closed, at least seven government offices have files on Pantani. In Forlì, he's tried and given a three-month suspension for what is termed "athletic fraud." But on appeal in Bologna, he is cleared because the legal accusation is technically invalid. In Trento, where he is also tried, he is likewise cleared because the accusation does not have legal merit.

In 2002 he races the Giro without leaving a mark. Unjustly, he is not invited to the Tour. Marco dismisses his disqualification for "possession of insulin," and his life begins a downward spiral leading to the devastation of his mind, heart, and spirit.

Pantani showed signs of his old fire at the 2003 Giro; it would be the final race of his life.

With great effort he returns to racing in 2003. His early preparation takes place in Spain, and he prepares well. Upon returning, he has success (second place) in a stage of the Coppi e Bartali stage race. At the Giro he seems like his old self on the Zoncolan, a climb similar in difficulty to the Mortirolo. He's third behind Gilberto Simoni and Garzelli, the strongest riders in the race. Marco is also able to make a good attack on the climb toward the Cascate del Toce. It's his last athletic achievement worthy of note. He is 14th overall in Milan.

After that, Marco's name comes up only in color commentaries. First the recovery in the Teolo (Padua) clinic, then two trips to Cuba, a slow distancing from everything around him, and a sad end in a little hotel in Rimini. He's alone, with his mind burning from dark thoughts and a deadly powder. He still has his heart and a few ounces of lucidity to write in his passport phrases that serve as an act of condemnation and a request for understanding. Marco dies on February 14, Valentine's Day like a bullfighter at *la cinco de la tarda*, and he now rests in the Cesenatico cemetery: Sector G, Niche 262, above the photo of Grandpa Sotero's smile, charismatic and compelling like his own.

On certain winter days, Cesenatico puts on a frozen mantle and appears in all of its contradictions. It was on such a day that Marco Pantani decided to launch his last breakaway on a climb much bigger than himself, much bigger than all of us.

Whoosh!
There Goes Pantani!

L'ALPE D'HUEZ, FRANCE *July 12, 1995*

EVERY TIME MARCO PANTANI ATTACKED during the 1994 Tour de France, he went too early or too late to merit a stage win. As a result, he collected a fistful of near-misses: third at Hautacam, second at Luz-Ardiden, eighth at L'Alpe d'Huez, and third at Val-Thorens. In 1995, his Carrera team is more attuned to Pantani's climbing talents. When a potentially stage-winning move emerges on the Col de la Croix de Fer—the second of stage 10's three giant, above-category climbs—Pantani's teammates Beat Zberg and Enrico Zaina (with coleader Claudio Chiappucci also in the group) join forces with Miguel Induráin's men to pursue a 13-man break. So instead of the attack reaching the foot of L'Alpe d'Huez with a probable five-minute margin, the gap is only one minute. And instead of being out of range, Pantani knows he has every chance of overtaking the break, even though it's led by six of the race's best climbers: Frenchmen Richard Virenque and Laurent Jalabert, Swiss Laurent Dufaux, Belgian Johan Bruyneel, Italian Ivan Gotti, and Spaniard Fernando Escartin.

Somebody once compared this Tour stage finish at L'Alpe d'Huez to another of the world's major sports events, the 100-meter dash at the Olympic Games. And with such outstanding contenders, this stage finish is like a Grand Prix of mountain climbing, although Pantani is starting with a one-minute handicap.

"I was focused on winning today," the shaven-headed Italian later admits. "But I was unsure of my form, and I didn't feel great at the bottom." He was unsure because a May 1 accident caused him to miss the Giro d'Italia and several weeks of training. But Pantani does know that he will have to make use of the steep, early part of the climb up the Alpe if he is going to catch the breakaway group. And so, less than a kilometer from the bottom, where the first of the 21 numbered switchback turns curves steeply to the right, the Carrera contender accelerates away from the Induráin group like a sprint runner taking a flyer from the starting blocks.

The ensuing 33 minutes of action are the most intense this Tour will see. Up ahead, the original break is splintering under an impressive surge from Gotti. And behind, after Pantani has departed on his upward mission, an intriguing exchange of hostilities develops between Bjarne Riis, Induráin, and Alex Zülle.

Despite the initial uncertainty about his form, Pantani is racing better than ever. His exciting climbing style—he alternates sprinting out of the saddle with longer, steadier, but still very fast pulls—quickly takes him to the front. Within 2 kilometers of his attack, the lithe Italian has charged up to the Virenque group, and then bridges to and immediately drops Gotti, who broke away from the lead group a kilometer earlier. With 10 kilometers of the spiraling climb still to go, Pantani is on his way to victory, with Gotti at 0:20; Jalabert, Virenque, and Escartin at 0:35; Riis at 0:52; Bruyneel at 1:05; and the seven-man Induráin group at 1:30.

Pantani displayed his "exciting climbing style" to take his first Alpe d'Huez stage win in 1995.

Watching this spectacular Alpe d'Huez assault are a couple of hundred thousand fans from all over Europe and the United States. ("I was surprised by how many Americans were on the mountain," enthuses Lance Armstrong, who is climbing the Alpe for the first time in his life.) Until 1994, the majority of L'Alpe d'Huez fans came from the Netherlands in response to the seemingly endless list of Dutch stage winners here. Replacing them in growing numbers are the Danes, waving their huge national flags in support of the inspired Riis, and Italians, particularly the different chapters of the Pantani Fan Club.

The Italians have a lot to cheer on this historic day, as Pantani continues to pull away to a splendid first Tour stage win. With 5 kilometers to go, Pantani's lead is 1:24. That's how it remains to the finish, where, before winning, he almost overshoots the last left turn.

The five-plus-hour alpine stage is decided in its final 35 minutes, the time in which Pantani transcends the other climbers and ascends the Alpe. "When I saw the climb I couldn't believe how steep it was," says Armstrong, who comes in 56th, 18:44 down on Pantani. "I guess that's why it has its reputation."

Indeed.

Alone on the Alpe

L'ALPE D' HUEZ, FRANCE *July 12, 1995*

A DIVINELY INSPIRED MOVIE DIRECTOR couldn't have thought up a worthier scene to pay homage to the best climber of modern cycling. The trajectory of that shaved head on a path that miraculously opened up before him in the middle of a sea of spectators is a movie frame that will remain etched in our memories: Pantani all alone on the mountain that the great Fausto Coppi of 1952 introduced to cycling, Pantani alone against the mountains like the great climbers of the past, and Pantani who takes off not knowing how long he can hold out, but who holds out—and how!

When his legs don't echo the sentiments of his head, Marco looks at the road as if it were the enemy. He no longer thinks about his opponents; he pedals against the physical pain. He clutches the handlebars and climbs, having nothing but contempt for his own fatigue. The anger is so intense, the desire to win so great, that he ends up almost flying into the barriers as he rounds the last turn within sight of the finish.

Marco had bade farewell to the yellow jersey group after the first slopes of L'Alpe d'Huez, then sucked up all of the breakaway riders like a vacuum

Pantani accelerated with 10 kilometers to go, just before dropping Ivan Gotti.

cleaner, without so much as a glance. The last to yield was Ivan Gotti, motivated in part by pride in the battle between generations. The rider from Bergamo held Marco's wheel for a single switchback, but that was it. The last 10 kilometers were reserved for the Romagnol with the shaved head and possessed eyes, and for no one else.

"Not a bad win, huh?" says a playful Pantani, who knows how to look at life with lucid coolness. "You may not believe me, but I didn't even know what I'd be able to accomplish. My left leg has my pulse constantly racing, and now I've caught something that is making my tongue swell up. I must have gotten a contaminated water bottle; I woke up this morning with my tongue all dry and covered with sores."

His *soigneur*, Roberto Pregnolato (the trainer who gave him the tattoos on his chest, one of a flower and the other of a butterfly), coated his tongue with an anti-inflammatory ointment before the start in Aime. Some sort of challenge is always dogging Pantani (he wanted to abandon the Tour four days earlier because of pain in his right knee), but when he sees a climb, he forgets about all of his problems.

"Yeah, that's the way it is," he explains. "I sat in until my attack on L'Alpe d'Huez. Zberg and Zaina did a great job limiting the gaps to the breakaway riders. I also saw that Chiappucci and I were on the same page in a way even I didn't think possible. After the initial slopes of the climb, something clicked that pushed me to attack, to attempt a display of force aimed at all of my competitors and at the mountain. It's the same thing that pushed me to attack last year on the Mortirolo, at Hautacam, on the Tourmalet, and also here at L'Alpe d'Huez. It's something bigger than myself. In moments like those, I'm not able to make calculations; I take off and see what happens."

Marco agilely spun his way (he was the only one using a 23-tooth cog) up the mountain to victory. "Once I was off on my own, I went for an exploit.

I'm not yet at my Pantani best; I'm not as strong as I was last year, but I don't think I rode any slower. More than my legs, it was grit, anger, and a desire to win that helped me. During the last 4 kilometers of the climb, I took a breather, then started pushing again, and kept repeating to myself, 'Come on, Marco, come on, the others can't go any faster than this.'"

Pantani is now seventh in the overall, 12:38 behind King Miguel. "Everything's still possible," he says. "Last year I came to win a stage and ended up on the podium. This year I'm shooting for the podium, and I've won a stage, perhaps the best one. I can already be satisfied, but not fulfilled."

Near-Miss in Colombia

DUITAMA, COLOMBIA *October 8, 1995*

ENCOURAGED BY HIS TWO MOUNTAINTOP STAGE WINS at the Tour de France and by a solid late-summer program of training and racing, Pantani headed to the 1995 world championships in Colombia with high hopes of success. He liked two features of the course: the city of Duitama's high base elevation of 8,300 feet and the total 14,000 feet of climbing over the 15 laps of the 17-kilometer circuit. Another favorable pointer for Pantani was the strength of the Italian national team, who acclimated to the high elevation by traveling early to South America. The *squadra*'s main leader was Gianni Bugno, who had already won two world championships, in 1991 and 1992, while Italy was one of only four teams that would start the seven-hour race in Colombia with the maximum 12 riders (the others were France, Spain, and the host nation).

Bugno was particularly confident. He came to Colombia at a mental and physical peak, and at the end of a season in which he had taken the Italian championship and second places in two World Cup classics. He even declared upon his arrival that he would not shave until he had taken his third title back to Italy. But Bugno soon showed signs of being overwhelmed by the media pressure put on him as the pre-race favorite. While training in the days before the October 8 race, his shock over the difficulty of the course led him to call for the Union Cycliste Internationale to reduce the race distance from 15 laps (265.5 kilometers) to 13 laps (230 kilometers). But without success. He then sought support from the French and Spanish teams in his request. And by the time the UCI threw out his claim, Bugno—a rider easily psyched out by adversity—had suffered a heavy blow to his morale.

All that pressure on Bugno enabled Pantani to prepare for the race in relative peace. He liked the course and the gracious inhabitants of this tourist-friendly community in the Andes. And he liked the fact that he could just focus on this one big day of racing.

The world professional road-race championship was the climax to a two-week spell of title racing. Throughout this period, the frenzy of the Colombian public had not faded. Hundreds of thousands of Colombians would line the road-race route at Duitama, reinforcing the general opinion that the 1995 event was the most popular for many years. "The crowds are great. I really appreciate the way they respond . . . not just to the stars, but to all the cyclists who are racing," said Spaniard Abraham Olano, who earlier in the week had finished second to his Spanish teammate, Miguel Induráin, in the 43-kilometer time-trial championship. Olano's thoughts were shared by many riders, for the cycling-wise masses extended their support to everyone, from the big names like Induráin, Bugno, and Pantani to little-known riders like the lone South African in the race, Dougie Ryder. For the latter they chanted, "Mandela . . . Mandela . . . " and sang choruses of the South African national anthem every time he passed.

But the biggest cheers were reserved for Induráin, who had won his record fifth consecutive Tour de France victory two months earlier. Rarely had a world championship started with a rider so fancied to win the race as the Spanish

The rivalry between Pantani and Induráin continued at the 1995 world's.

giant. He had benefitted from his fine-toothed preparation in the high eleva-
tions of Colorado in the weeks preceding the world's, and then his victory over
Olano in the world time-trial championship four days before the road race.
These placed a tidal wave of pressure on Induráin to come up with the goods.

AFTER HEAVY OVERNIGHT SHOWERS had swamped Duitama and its surrounding ter-
rain, the field was content to let Frenchman Laurent Roux slip away on the first
of 15 laps. While the Frenchman stayed out on his own for the opening four
hours, the race pace was demanding from the get-go. The big teams rode at a
tempo that saw riders drop off the back one by one—even on the first lap. But
what shocked everyone was two-time world champion Bugno's abandonment

of the race after only five laps. The image of his unshaven face hanging in his hands, as he sat in the Italian pit area after dropping out, confirmed how tough the circuit truly was. Italian hopes now lay with Pantani and his teammate Claudio Chiappucci.

The start of the *real* proceedings was symbolically heralded by a crack of thunder, as a storm crept over the Andes from the north, during the eighth lap. At the summit of the main climb and with 133 kilometers covered, early attacker Roux was still in front by three minutes. But his moment of glory was brought to an end on the next lap. Almost as soon as Roux was caught, a four-man break counterattacked on the steep descent. In it were Italy's Chiappucci and Gianni Faresin, along with Spain's Francisco Mauleon and Colombia's José "Chepe" Gonzalez. This break had a 26-second lead going into lap 10, and was 36 seconds in front before being brought back on the climb by the Spanish-led peloton. Another break quickly formed, composed of Mauleon, Russia's Dmitri Konyshev, Denmark's Rolf Sørensen, Colombia's Israel Ochoa, and Italy's Paolo Lanfranchi. This group had a 35-second lead at the end of the lap, with 177 kilometers now completed. A sign of the fast pace was confirmed by the tenth lap's average speed of 37.704 kilometers per hour— remarkable for a lap that contained almost 1,000 feet of climbing.

Konyshev and Ochoa dropped their companions on the eleventh lap, and then combined forces brilliantly to take a 1:25 lead on the Italian-led pack at the summit. It was here and now that the looming storm finally broke through and the heavens opened over Duitama.

The storm, the chases from behind, and the rapid, slippery descent added to the nervousness of the peloton. And that mood was deepened by the spectacular crash on the descent of Colombia's Juan Ramirez, who collided with a parked ambulance. Pantani's teammate Chiappucci also fell, and he would drop out on the following lap. His and Bugno's absence were a blow to Pantani's chances.

Meanwhile, Konyshev and Ochoa's lead was under threat, and after starting lap 12 with 33 seconds on the diminished main group, they were quickly brought back. Sixty kilometers remained and the world title was still up for grabs.

The first major contender to show his hand was Pantani. Despite his tires sliding on the wet uphill, Marco attacked fiercely out of the main group, which was down to only 20 riders. But Pantani's effort was marked by Ochoa, Konyshev, and Spain's José Maria Jimenez, while five others tagged on later. Perhaps Pantani achieved the situation he wanted. He was clear with just eight other riders: Induráin, Olano, Jimenez, and Fernando Escartin from Spain; Mauro Gianetti, Pascal Richard, and Felice Puttini from Switzerland; and Oliverio Rincon from Colombia. The biggest problem for Pantani was the lack of any teammates, but fellow Italian Francesco Casagrande eventually made it back to the nine leaders, along with Frenchman Richard Virenque and a few others.

At the same time, on the descent Puttini went on the offensive for the Swiss; he was joined by Spain's Escartin. This pair took a 30-second lead and held it through the thirteenth lap. Their respective teammates were still in the majority in the group behind, now numbering 16 riders, so it would be up to the other nations to launch a counterattack. But as they tackled the main climb for the penultimate time, Escartin and Puttini ran out of juice and the race became a street fight. Colombia's Gonzalez threw the first punch, a move countered by Spain's Jimenez, who was seemingly bestowed with endless strength. Switzerland's Gianetti followed them. Meanwhile, local hero Rincon halted because of a puncture and had to pull out all stops to rejoin the leaders.

TWO-THIRDS OF THE WAY UP the hill, just as the shrunken lead group of eight riders accelerated, a flat tire tested the patience of the man still favored to win the race: Induráin. Up to this point, the Spaniard had barely been in difficulty, other than a puncture midway through the race. This second flat came at a far more critical moment.

The urgency for quick neutral support was paramount. Realizing that a wheel change would take too long, Induráin threw his bike to the ground and grabbed a spare. He then powered away on a false flat preceding the steep 1-kilometer pitch to the summit to get back with the leaders. But, as impressive as his pursuit had been, Induráin wasn't at ease; he kept his plight secret to all but Olano. "After I changed bikes," he said, "I just couldn't get the right sensation back in my legs."

> "I took advantage of the flat," he later admitted. "I knew the last climb would be very difficult." And it was.

Still, Induráin wanted to try his hand at a winning attack . . . and his moment came just before the summit. With his 174-pound torso rising from the saddle like a wave about to crash, all he needed to do was get a gap on his rivals and milk the descent of all its speed. However, the Russian Konyshev jumped onto Induráin's wheel, and Pantani and the others soon followed. The ball was back in the court of the numerically superior Spanish, and they bided their time until after the descent to make the next move. It came from Olano. Sensing that his prowess was on the flat, rather than the final uphill stretch, Olano bolted out from the group with 21 kilometers to go.

Induráin, leading the group, didn't flinch a bit. He glanced to his right and was met by a wall of stares from Richard, Virenque, Pantani, Konyshev, and

Rincon. Induráin reacted similarly after his other teammate, Escartin, momentarily sped away from the group early into the last lap. Ahead, Olano was committed to a gold medal–seeking ride. And he realized that the key to his aspirations hinged on his taking as much time as possible while the others hesitated. "I took advantage of the flat," he later admitted. "I knew the last climb would be very difficult." And it was.

Olano tackled the final ascent at an even tempo, rather aggressively. "I started to feel a cramp coming on, so I eased up a little," he later revealed. "But then I think that helped me keep some reserves for a strong finish." Meanwhile, as Induráin's rivals remained hesitant, the chase group saw a half dozen riders reconnect, but not for long. The first part of the final ascent saw five men emerge from the group behind Olano: Pantani, Induráin, Richard, Puttini, and Virenque—although the last two were soon dropped.

This was perhaps Pantani's last chance to break up the Spanish grip on the race. But the wet roads again forced the little Italian to stay in the saddle. His wheels started to spin on the slick surface when he tried to stand on the pedals. Meanwhile, Induráin loyally sat on Pantani's wheel, half expecting a counterattack from Richard, which he was ready to follow. "I thought Richard would attack. He was the one I feared the most," said Induráin, describing the moment that might have opened the last door to his winning the world title. "But then I looked around and saw he had gone; the only Swiss rider left was Gianetti."

With a daring descent to the flat homestretch, Pantani tried once more to close the gap on Olano. But it proved impossible, given the presence of a still-powerful Induráin. The race appeared to be sealed for Olano until he punctured with 2 kilometers to go. The Spaniard's rear wheel started to buckle; fate seemed to have turned against him, and perhaps in favor of Pantani. Olano didn't have time to stop and change the wheel or his bike; he just had to pray that the rim wouldn't crack. As rain fell and thunder bellowed over Duitama, someone from above must have taken time out to bless Olano, in what would be remembered as one of the most exciting finales to a world championship.

Olano continued to ride furiously toward the finish line on his flat tire as Pantani and Gianetti chased, with Induráin on their tail. "I knew I had punctured," said Olano. "But I didn't think of anything except to get to the finish as quickly as possible. I knew that they could come back on me." But they didn't.

Olano was elated as he crossed the line, 35 seconds ahead of the chasers. The sprint for the silver medal went to Induráin. As he outsped Pantani and Gianetti, Induráin's ferocious gesture of joy—a swing of his right hand, which he then punched into the air—said it all. Later he confirmed, "I am happy with my second place . . . or rather, for the way I finished second. The whole team was great, and what's important is that we have taken the win."

As he awaited the medal ceremony, Pantani knew that he would never again have such an opportunity to win the world's.

If Chiappucci hadn't crashed or Bugno had not crumbled, then that world championship might have gone to Pantani, not Olano. The fact that the Italian would never again have such a great chance to win cycling's supreme title was reflected in Pantani's look of despair as he sat alone awaiting the medal ceremony. He came to the Andes looking for gold but had to settle for bronze.

Marco on the
March Again

L'ALPE D'HUEZ, FRANCE *July 19, 1997*

NOT MUCH WENT RIGHT FOR MARCO PANTANI after he earned his bronze medal at the 1985 world championships. In his first race back in Europe, just ten days after the world's in Colombia, he was racing downhill into Turin, 4 kilometers from the finish of the Milan-Turin race, when he and two other riders collided with an oncoming Jeep that had eluded police outriders on the closed course. Pantani suffered the most serious injuries; the multiple fractures of his left leg were so severe that many observers thought his budding career could be over. But after several surgeries and months of rehab, he began racing again in August 1996. It was another nine months, however, before he became competitive when another, thankfully less serious, crash eliminated him from the Giro d'Italia. So there were still serious doubts that he would be able to return to the sport's top level when, six weeks after the Giro crash, he began the 1997 Tour de France.

After Pantani came in third and second on the Tour's first two mountain stages in the Pyrenees, he headed to the Alps, convinced that his best form was close. His fans also sensed their hero's imminent return, and they traveled in thousands across the border, ready to salute a Pantani victory for the first time in two years. Among the Italians who camped out on the mountainside for a couple of days before the Alpe d'Huez stage was Pantani's father, who knew how much his son had suffered during the long months of physical therapy after his October 1995 accident.

Going into the thirteenth stage, starting in St. Etienne, Pantani was lying in fifth place overall, an enormous 9:11 behind race leader Jan Ullrich, but only a minute behind Spain's Abraham Olano in third place. A podium finish was still possible.

Given Ullrich's commanding overall lead—almost six minutes on runner-up Richard Virenque of Festina—the German's Telekom team employed rather strange tactics on the stage. The whole team pulled the pack at 50 kilometers per hour for the last, gradual uphill 15 kilometers in the valley preceding the Alpe d'Huez climb. It was as if they were headed toward a field sprint rather than the Tour's most challenging mountaintop finish. The only logical explanation was that Telekom captain Bjarne Riis and team director Walter Godefroot believed that this was the only way to make sure Ullrich was at the front of the pack to start the infamous 21-switchback ascent.

If the hard pace was designed to tire the climbers' legs before the Alpe, it only partly worked. Festina's Pascal Hervé took up the pace around the first switchback, turn 21, with teammate Virenque on his wheel, followed by a small group headed by Ullrich. As Hervé dropped back, Virenque surged. Ullrich was quickly on his rival's wheel, along with Italy's Francesco Casagrande, Riis, and Pantani.

In blazing sunshine, Pantani had already thrown his racing cap to the ground. And now he threw down his challenge, just before the second switchback, turn 20, where the grade is more than 10 percent. The Italian powered to the front, Virenque went with him, and Ullrich and Riis were the only others who could follow. Pantani was riding with strength and fluidity, often on the drops and out of the saddle, and repeatedly accelerating. "I never worried about the others," said the confident Italian. "I planned to ride at the front . . . and drop them one by one."

And that's just what happened. Ten minutes into the climb, Riis simply couldn't maintain the high pace any longer. Two minutes later, Virenque fell back. "I preferred to climb at my own pace, rather than risk exploding," said the Frenchman in the polka-dot jersey. And then, another half minute later, Ullrich, too, had to drop off Pantani's wheel, as the Italian accelerated into a steep right hairpin curve. Only one third of the climb had been completed.

> "I never worried about the others," said the confident Italian. "I planned to ride at the front . . . and drop them one by one."

The big question to be asked at this point was: Why did Ullrich chase Pantani so hard? Surely he wasn't expecting to win the stage. So why was he concerned about a rider more than nine minutes behind him in the general classification? Perhaps the Telekom team really did think Pantani posed a threat to Ullrich's yellow jersey in the three days of climbing through the Alps. But their immediate challenger was Virenque, so if Ullrich had simply stayed with the Frenchman, the German would have had a much easier ride—and perhaps still ridden away from Virenque before the finish. Instead, the race leader was expending huge amounts of energy, showing his inexperience, and even risking blowing up.

At the front, Pantani was being urged on by huge crowds, estimated at half a million people. He couldn't see the *Vai Pirata* and *Forza Pantani* banners, but he could hear the excited cheers of his fans, including those of Papà

Pantani was ecstatic when he won at l'Alpe d'Huez for the second time—it was his first big victory since breaking his leg.

Pantani, only inches from his face. Pantani had to push two rabid fans out of the way when they got too close. Still, this is where he wanted to be. "Once I was alone, I had the most motivation to win the stage," Pantani said. "I know this course very well, and it plays to my strengths."

No one, not even Ullrich, was as strong as Pantani on this particular day. The Mercatone Uno leader was climbing at record pace, mostly turning a gear of 39x17, although he said he used a 16-tooth sprocket on the "easier" parts and a 19 when the grade was at its steepest. With 5 kilometers still to climb—and the ski resort on the mountaintop now in clear view—Pantani was 25 seconds ahead of Ullrich, 47 up on Virenque, and 1:52 on Riis and Casagrande. The gaps continued to grow.

Into the town and onto a flatter stretch, Pantani shifted to the big ring and stayed with it around the final turn to race out of the saddle all the way to the line. He had completed the 14.5-kilometer climb in a record 37:35, an average climbing speed of 23.148 kilometers per hour, breaking his own 1994 record by 25 seconds. The clock showed he had beaten Ullrich by 47 seconds, Virenque by 1:27, and Casagrande and Riis by 2:27. Pantani's gains saw him leapfrog Riis into third place overall, while Olano, finishing 3:25 back, fell to fifth.

Marco Pantani was again the toast of the Tour. He did the rounds of media interviews before ending up at the after-stage show on French TV. Awaiting him there was one very happy father, who gave his son a big kiss. They both knew that the good times were back.

Pantani alone on a mountain climb—here at the 1994 Giro d'Italia—soon became a familiar sight.

At the 1995 Tour de France, Pantani won stages in
sunshine at L'Alpe d'Huez (top) and in thick fog at
Guzet-Neige (bottom).

In his first big race after breaking his left leg, Pantani put the hurt on race leader Jan Ullrich (in yellow) and runner-up Richard Virenque at the 1997 Tour.

A critical moment in the 1998 Giro: After discarding his diamond jewelry, Pantani left behind his final rival, the Russian Pavel Tonkov, on the brutal climb to Montecampione.

As he headed to victory at the 1998 Giro, Pantani was often alone with his thoughts.

Pantani clinched the 1998 Tour with third place in the final time trial (right) before celebrating with teammate Fabiano Fontanelli on the Champs-Élysées in Paris (below).

With support from his Mercatone Uno team, Pantani comfortably defended the yellow jersey in the final days of the 1998 Tour.

At the 1999 Giro, Pantani dashed to one of his four mountaintop stage wins prior to losing the leader's pink jersey after an above-the-limit blood test.

The Captain
and His Crew

COURCHEVEL, FRANCE *July 20–21, 1997*

THIS IS THE STORY OF A LONG NIGHT, a very long night. It's the eve of the Morzine stage of the 1997 Tour de France. Marco Pantani is not feeling well after his victory at L'Alpe d'Huez: He has an ugly cough. The Pirate is ready to quit and return home, but his teammate Marcello Siboni is with him keeping watch through these seemingly endless hours.

It's a battle that even Siboni thinks he will lose. He understands that Pantani really means it when he says, "I'm going home," between bouts of coughing that seem to shatter his chest. It isn't the words, but the cough that makes Siboni understand the real danger of Marco's imminent desertion. The previous day, Pantani won on the Alpe, but today is different. Everything has changed, just as the sky suddenly changes in the mountains. Yesterday the sun was shining. Today the sky is a deadly gray. And it is cold.

In their hotel room at Courchevel, Siboni repeats many times to his friend that Morzine is the finish of tomorrow's stage. "Marco, it's the Morzine stage. The one you've been telling me for months you want to win, because after the last climb there is a long downhill run, and you want to show you can win even at the end of a descent, not only at the top of a mountain climb. Marco, don't you remember?"

Marco is coughing, but he remembers very well that Morzine is the stage he has most dreamed of—more than L'Alpe d'Huez, which, after all, he had won in the past. But he is coughing constantly and his face turns red as a beet because he can't breathe, and he keeps saying, "I'm going home . . . enough . . . I'm going home."

So on this cold evening at Courchevel, high in the French Alps, Siboni decides to go down and look for his veteran teammate Roberto Conti, to give him a hand, because Pantani is serious. He is threatening to quit, and perhaps he has already made up his mind.

CONTI HAS AN AUTHORITATIVE VOICE. He is the man Pantani had at his side that entire day, after the lightning attack by a formidable Festina team. Richard Virenque's squad had preplanned a mass breakout to put race leader Jan Ullrich on the ropes. They had worked well, surprising even those who had known about the plan.

As they gathered at the day's start, Siboni had told Conti about the plan. "I smell something burning," he said. "Today's stage is a short one, and you'll see a battle."

In fact, Virenque lined up his men and attacked less than 10 kilometers into the stage. The blow struck the target immediately. Ullrich was caught in the net, and if his Telekom team captain, Bjarne Riis, hadn't been there to help him out, perhaps the German would have lost control of the Tour. He was frightened and lost in the intricacy of a race that had suddenly become too

Roberto Conti (right) was both a teammate and close friend of his "captain" Pantani.

complicated for his 23 years. But Riis gave him a formidable hand, and little by little the Virenque attack fell apart.

Pantani, meanwhile, remained behind. He was already suffering from acute bronchitis, made worse by the frigid weather after his triumph at the Alpe. There had been celebrations: All of Cesenatico seemed to be up there to greet him, and he was in the crowd with a lot of happiness to work off. The sun was shining . . . but then it turned cold.

AT THE COURCHEVEL HOTEL, Siboni finds Conti's room and they start talking.

"You have to come, Roberto," says Siboni. "Come to Marco and see if you can convince him. He wants to go home."

Conti says not to despair. "He says that now, but then he'll go to sleep, and tomorrow he'll be ready to race."

"No, it's not that simple," Siboni replies. "The situation has taken a bad turn. We need you, Roberto."

This solidarity of purpose, a fraternal dependence experienced by a team's racers, sometimes in dramatic circumstances, is the essence of true bicycle racing, a sport that is true to its traditions. In the middle of exhausting efforts and in the crucial moments of an adventure that can become desperate, solidarity blossoms and the group takes the measure of its strength.

Conti and Siboni go up to join Pantani. It is not hard for Conti to understand that Pantani is indeed very sick. A racer, and one as experienced as Conti, who is in his twelfth season as a cycling professional, can hear the harshness of Marco's cough. He knows that being too optimistic isn't the best tactic in these circumstances, but he nonetheless says to Marco, "You'll feel better tomorrow. Get a good night's sleep."

Conti then goes on to plea on behalf of the boys who had worked so hard for him in the first two weeks of the Tour. "Marco, I can see that you are ill," Conti says, "but hang in there. Do it for us. All our efforts have been centered on you. With our assistance, we can still help you take third in the classification, and we'll take home some real money, the prizes to share. Think about it, Marco. We'll stick close to you."

Conti winks at Siboni. Pantani doesn't reply but makes it clear he has understood and is ready to give his all to get a good rest. Conti nudges Siboni and indicates with his head that they are to leave. In the corridor, they spend a half hour talking.

"I say he will leave the race, but don't you say anything to him." Conti tells Siboni, who shares the room with Pantani. "And stay near him. If you need help during the night, call me."

The night is never-ending. Pantani sleeps a little and coughs a little. Siboni, in part because of the noise and in part because of his tension and real fear that Marco will abandon the Tour, does not sleep at all.

Like Conti, Siboni, 33, is a seasoned rider, although he has never won a race in his 11 years as a professional. He hails from Cesena, about 15 kilometers from where Pantani lives on the Adriatic coast. He is Pantani's most trusted and greatest friend, the one who makes sure, for Marco's sake, that harmony reigns on the team. Siboni says, "Marco takes off in higher spirits if his teammates are optimistic and ready to help. That's how he is. He needs the comfort of his group. He is a real *capo*, demanding and at the same time generous."

Virenque and Ullrich were the last riders to stay with Pantani on the Joux-Plane climb.

THE FEARED "NEXT MORNING" FINALLY COMES, and Pantani feels a little better. He is breathing more evenly and coughing less. And thankfully, he wants to prove he can win at Morzine. "He has been telling me for months he could do it," says Siboni. "Ever since the winter, when we went training together before the Giro. I understood when he made certain experimental moves. He would suddenly spurt ahead on a climb. Those were the days when, after his horrific accident at Turin, he didn't even know whether he would ever go back to bike racing."

Ironically, it's Siboni who is not feeling well in the stage to Morzine. "In truth, *I* was the one on the verge of pulling out," he says. "Me. The one who had given Marco my soul to make sure he would go on despite the bronchitis. I was dead beat because, not having slept, I was destroyed even before the start."

Six alpine climbs, including two Category 1 passes and the hors-category Col de Joux-Plane, were on the menu for the fifteenth stage. Although there wasn't a from-the-gun battle like the day before, the end result was similar, with only 46 riders finishing within 20 minutes of the stage winner. Those 46 riders made up the front group after climbing the Croix-Fry and Colombière passes in quick succession.

The Festina team set the pace on the long descent, and again went into action to chase down a two-man break on the flat valley floor leading to Samoëns. This is where they started the final climb, the Joux-Plane, which averages 10 percent for most of its 12 kilometers. The group grew smaller with every kilometer, until only 11 riders were left at the front going into the second half of the climb. Riis then took over the tempo for Ullrich until, moments later, Pantani attacked. The group exploded and the Italian quickly raced away from five chasers.

Pantani was soon out of sight and gaining 10 seconds every kilometer. Even so, Virenque still had hopes of another stage win, and he made repeated accelerations until only Ullrich was left on his wheel. At the summit, Pantani was 55 seconds ahead of his two pursuers. And amazingly, the slightly built climber continued to gain time on the 9-kilometer descent to win the stage by 1:17 over Virenque and Ullrich.

It was quite a day for Pantani, who only that morning had been talking of pulling out of the Tour because of his bronchitis. The Italian climber not only took his second stage in three days, but he also regained third place on overall time.

Marco won the Morzine stage and showed his team that he was captain.

The Morzine stage had given Pantani proof of his rebirth and showed people that real champions can overcome the highest obstacles. Siboni, half dead from fatigue, joins his team leader in their camper van, and Pantani warmly embraces him, saying, "What class I have. Did you see?"

It is a way of emphasizing the event after the previous evening's fear and the cough that tormented him all night. Siboni smiles—he doesn't have the strength to do anything else. Then he lays a hand on Pantani's shoulder, which in truth he should have heartily thumped in the manner of all people from Romagna, showing that he indeed had been amazing. They understand each other perfectly. A week later, the Tour over, they were back training together. The story of that gray day and black night, placed by destiny between two happier days, becomes one that fills their moments between the fatigue of a climb and the enjoyment of a good glass of wine.

Siboni, naturally, is the confidant. He is the friend, the workmate of Pantani, the person with whom you might not exchange a word for hours on end, but who understands you as if you had been conversing at great length. Siboni knows everything about Pantani and laughs at what he reads in the newspapers, sometimes things that are complete fantasy.

"Is it true," the fans ask him, "that now Pantani wants to train for the time trial?"

"Don't be ridiculous," Siboni laughs. "He isn't stupid. If anything, he will be building his strength to pedal faster uphill."

"And is it true," they ask, never tiring of wanting to know, "that in the Pyrenees during the Tour he was humiliated because he didn't win a stage?"

"Not so," Siboni replies patiently. "In the Pyrenees, he was very angry, not because he hadn't won, but because he had not been able to shake off Virenque. That was his obsession. He told me that many times."

"What?" the fans insist, carried away by the champion's little secrets.

"He would say to me, 'If that guy bothers me, I'll kick up such a row that a bunch of them will be going home.' And then he added, 'Keep your eyes open. I'm going to attack when nobody expects it.'"

That was Pantani, the man who made the boys in the team go crazy with joy, who took away the pain of their fatigue, and who made his guardian angel, Siboni, understand that he was the captain.

Consecration

CESENATICO *June 8, 1998*

AN ANGELIC SMILE FORMED ON THAT DEVILISH FACE when the *maglia rosa* was slipped onto his small, slim Popsicle stick of a body. Marco Pantani stared straight ahead, zipped up the pink jersey, and climbed onto the podium's top step to the cheers of his fans. For several minutes his faithful chanted, "*Numero uno! Numero uno! Numero uno!*"

When he's focused, *Il Pirata* has a mean look that tells the story of the troubled path that has brought him to this point. He seems much more mature than the typical 28-year-old. But when he smiles, he becomes a child. "I earned this jersey. It was a victory of will. I even defeated fate," he says, thinking of the hospital bed in Turin in October 1995, his left leg broken in two places. "It would have been easier to say, 'Okay, I give up.' I came out of that experience stronger. I came to understand what it means to cope, what the word 'determination' means. My friends and my father, who suffered along with me, helped me a lot. Now I look at life and sports differently."

No one can say what Pantani the athlete would be like if it hadn't been for that infamous accident in Milan-Turin. "It's impossible to grasp. One of my

"Numero uno, numero uno," *chanted the fans when Pantani won the 1998 Giro d'Italia.*

legs is now almost a centimeter shorter," he says. "In 1994 I wanted to see what my limits were. I had won two stages at the Giro, putting myself in second place after dropping Induráin on the Mortirolo. At the Tour I had finished on the podium. Then between car accidents and various cats, I haven't been able to race a complete season."

The evolution of his career has gone in spurts, like his attacks in the mountains. Like the one at Plan di Montecampione on stage 19 of the 1998 Giro d'Italia, the "triumph or die" attack, the one in which he tossed the diamond from his nose-piercing into the trees. "I had my nose pierced and put that little diamond in it on New Year's Eve. It was a tangible symbol that I didn't want to be told what to do by anything or anyone. It was a way for me to say, 'I'll do whatever I want.' It was there to symbolize my pride. After the sign that marked 3 kilometers to the finish, and before what I felt would be the last possible place to attack, I heard a voice that said, 'Throw it, throw it away.' It wasn't an earthly voice."

> "I heard a voice that said, 'Throw it, throw it away.' It wasn't an earthly voice."

Runner-up Pavel Tonkov raised some suspicion about Pantani's third place in the final time trial. "I shouldn't even respond to these provocations. I won my Giro fair and square. Whoever claims the contrary is dishonest. And I don't think those were Tonkov's own words, because he never says anything. Pavel knows I won this Tour by undermining his ambitions in the mountains. He was a tough, an excellent, opponent, but I don't think there can be any doubt: I earned the *maglia rosa* more than anyone else. Pavel's victory would have been one of mediocrity. He would have betrayed courage and fantasy in favor of benefiting from the work of others, following wheels."

Pantani produced the best time trial of his career in Lugano at the end of the Giro. "You might not believe this, but I've got better legs now than when we left Nice on the first day. But in the time trial, the thing that made the difference was my determination. I thought the entire night before the time trial about the 1989 Tour finish, when Laurent Fignon lost the yellow jersey by eight seconds to Greg LeMond. 'That won't happen to me,' I thought. It would have been terrible. I didn't want to lose. I just couldn't lose." Did he ever struggle? "After the stage 15 time trial in Trieste I had my doubts. When Alex Zülle passed me, it threw me off. That humiliation was hard to swallow, but I made him pay for it, and then some."

On the day of the final victory, *Il Pirata* remembered a great personality: "Above all, I want to dedicate this *maglia rosa* to myself, because I fought tooth and nail for it, always believing I could do it. But I would also like to make mention of Luciano Pezzi, the wisest member of our entire team. Luciano wasn't able to be here at the Giro, but he was here by way of telephone and faxes. He was the great mediator who addressed our issues; some of the credit goes to him."

Russian rider Pavel Tonkov (left) was Pantani's biggest rival at the 1998 Giro.

Pantani is more than captain of the Mercatone Uno–Bianchi team. He *is* the Mercatone Uno–Bianchi team. His teammates, the team managers, the mechanics, and the *soigneurs* had all completely shaved their heads before the final stage into Milan. Alberto Mancusi, the barber from Senago, shaved the heads of 22 people, late into Saturday night. And the day before, the whole clan had shown up with their shaved heads, wearing T-shirts that read, "Mission accomplished." And what gift does Marco want to give himself? "Just some partying as soon as I get home," he said. "I already gave myself the gift. This *maglia rosa* is an immense joy. It's about more than just athletics. It's as if life were giving something back that it had previously denied me."

When *Il Pirata* returns to Cesenatico, he finds a town in celebration. "It makes me extremely happy; I love my people," he says. "But I would also like to enjoy a little peace and quiet. If the stores hadn't been closed, I would have gone to San Marino to buy a big box of Viagra and would have closed all the doors and windows for a few days. . . . Hey, I'm just kidding!"

MARCO BITES INTO THE FLATBREAD with the voracity of a child returning from a day of adventure. The flatbread isn't filled with creamy, chocolatey Nutella, his favorite; it's a classic flatbread wrap with cooked prosciutto and mozzarella. It's already evening, but *Il Pirata* woke up just a little while ago and has come by the family concession stand for a Romagnese "breakfast." This irresistible food stand, the white-and-green stripes of which resemble Team Kelme's graphics, has become a cult cycling destination. Even bike tourists get in line, remembering Mamma Tonina's motto: *"Con piadine e crescioni si fanno i campioni"* ("Champions are made with flatbread and watercress"). Not that the diet works for everyone. Pantani's teammate Marcello Siboni is also giving it a try, but with all due respect.

At Mamma Tonina's stand, these are festive times. Over the past few days, sister Manola and Christina, Marco's fiancée, have served more than a thousand flatbread wraps, from 9 A.M. until 2 A.M. Production slowed only in the late afternoon, when all eyes were glued to the TV. Manola's pink hair says it all. Papà Paolo exposes his head: he had been completely buzzed in Lugano on the night of the mass shavings.

Marco Pantani bites into his flatbread and waves to his old friends. He doesn't have much of a voice, like someone who has just gotten up. His first day as winner of the Giro d'Italia has been bigger than it has been long. After the grand finale in Milan, Pantani celebrates at the ristorante Ribot with his clan and the team's sponsors. He gets on the microphone to thank everyone, one by one, and for many it opens the floodgate of tears. Then he is off, back to the coast.

"I arrived in Cesenatico around one in the morning. My friends were still at the Bar dei Pini; that's sort of my club's meeting place. They set off some fireworks, and then I enjoyed the night with my friends. My fiancée, Christina, was a bit annoyed, but she knows me by now." Pantani's night ends at the Bar dei Marinai at 6:30 in the morning with a cappuccino in front of him. He "partied like an animal," as he had promised himself he would. "Friends are important to me. They are at the top of my list of what's important." Only with them is Marco able to be completely himself, without obligations or conditions.

After three weeks of tension, Pantani now yearns for his quiet port and the paths along the Canale di Leonardo. "I experienced my most intense emotions on the roads of the Giro, when I heard the fans yell 'Pantani' so much that it gave me a headache," he says. "For me, coming home is synonymous with tranquillity. It's a bit like laying down your weapons, like taking off your armor. It's rest for the warrior. Now I feel like relieving the stress by riding alone for a few days on my own inland roads. Then I'll think about the rest of the season."

Pantani's Giro win made him Italy's most popular sports star—everyone wanted to touch him.

The rest of the season means, above all, the Tour de France. "My objectives will be directly tied to the team's plans. I'll only think about my ambitions for the Tour de France in a couple of weeks."

Pantani often talks about the team's plans because he has had a few run-ins with the management of Mercatone Uno. "My teammates were exceptional; I

Marco rode the strongest time trial of his career to clinch victory at the 1998 Giro.

can't even find adjectives that could aptly describe the hard work, the generosity of people like Massimo Podenzana and Roberto Conti," he says. "But I've been anxious for about two months now, because there are some cogs that need a little oil. There were things about the management of our team that were baffling. Some things, including those that affect morale, still need to be resolved."

Marco Pantani is currently the champion with the best quality-to-price ratio—it's said he makes about half a million dollars per year, quite a bit less than the other stars, like Jan Ullrich. All of the world's best teams are knocking on Pantani's door. But, he says, "This is my group, a machine that is off to a good start. If a cog isn't working, you don't have to throw away the whole machine, you just need to change the cog." There are some things that are bothering Pantani, but he doesn't want to be more explicit. For now, he prefers to enjoy this moment of great popularity.

In winning the Giro, *Il Pirata* has even eclipsed Italian soccer for popularity, just days before the start of the 1998 World Cup. "I hope that all of the wonderful attention that cycling is currently getting will positively affect the entire sport," he comments. "I hope that I'm not the only one to benefit from it. I hope that today or tomorrow some little kids will already be choosing cycling as their sport. Now I'm even more aware that I have responsibilities. During the Lago Lacena stage in the opening week, 'Pantani' was written on the road in all different colors for at least 3 kilometers. And that writing will be there for at least a year. It had a certain effect on me, but it doesn't scare me. When I was in that hospital bed in Turin, I realized that you can lose everything in an instant, but that you can never stop believing. When you really believe in something, you'll achieve it in the end."

Above the Storm

THICK CLOUDS CLOAKING ICE-LINED PEAKS, suddenly unleashing sheets of bone-numbing rain. A solo cyclist, his teeth clacking, body shaking, red-raw hands gripping levers like a leech as he gropes his way down a mountainside through thick fog. Swollen waterfalls, thousands of feet high, cascade down jet-black cliffs, filling rivers in a glacial, white-gray fury. A whistling, gusting wind catches a rider sideways as, trying to don a rain jacket, he navigates a series of steep, downhill switchbacks. Another rider, hypothermic, is lifted from his bike by spectators, taken into a house, and given cups of steaming hot chocolate before a doctor arrives.

These are images from a day of drama, when a confluence of extreme conditions, competitiveness, and courage produced a mythic stage of the 1998 Tour de France. Such stages come along perhaps once in a decade. One that comes to mind is the Gavia stage of the 1988 Giro d'Italia, when the combination of a blizzard, a terrifying descent on dirt roads, and epic racing saw American Andy Hampsten take over the leader's pink jersey. But perhaps the only postwar Tour stage to which this one can be compared is the one between

Briançon and Aix-les-Bains in 1958. That day, in almost identical stormy weather and on some of the same roads, Frenchman Raphaël Geminiani lost the yellow jersey after Luxembourger Charly Gaul, known as the Angel of the Mountains, made an 80-kilometer breakaway over the Luitel, Porte, Cucheron, and Granier climbs to overcome an overnight deficit of ten minutes.

The epic rides of Gaul and the Italian legends, Fausto Coppi and Gino Bartali, were things Marco Pantani learned about from the older members of his first cycling club in Cesenatico. When Pantani got hold of Gaul's address in the winter of 1997–1998, he drove to Luxembourg and spoke for hours with the 1958 Tour winner. The two became fast friends, and Gaul now sends Pantani messages of encouragement and visits with him at the big races.

Asked why he hadn't bothered to check it out in training before this year's race, Ullrich said, "Sometimes it's best not to see where the end is."

No doubt Gaul had told the Italian climber about the 1958 Tour and how he won the race in the Alps. The question now was: Could Pantani repeat Gaul's deeds of 40 years earlier? The answer to that question would surely hinge on what would be the hardest, highest mountain pass of the race: the Télégraphe-Galibier combination, which is effectively a single climb, rising more than 6,500 feet in 30 kilometers. The early slopes of the Galibier, as the road leaves the small tourist town of Valloire and heads upward with an initial 12 percent pitch, is where many a Tour has taken a decisive turn. The last time the race came this way, in 1993, a break by Tony Rominger, Miguel Induráin, Alvaro Mejia, and Andy Hampsten decided the Tour's final result.

The 1996 Tour was also slated to come this way, but snow, subfreezing temperatures, and gale-force winds led the race organizers to cancel the climb. Instead the riders went over the Galibier in team cars, and that was the only time the current race leader and defending champion Jan Ullrich had seen this road. Asked why he hadn't bothered to check it out in training before this year's race, Ullrich said, "Sometimes it's best not to see where the end is."

On that July day in 1998, three men—the Italian Rodolfo Massi, Frenchman Christophe Rinero, and Spaniard Marcos Serrano—slipped ahead and survived the mist-shrouded Télégraphe ascent to hit the Galibier with a healthy gap. They were then joined by another Spaniard, José Maria Jimenez. This was the background to what would produce the most decisive moments of the 1998 Tour.

Through the slashing rain, the main group, now climbing the Galibier at a faster tempo, grew smaller by the minute. Then, about 10 kilometers from the top, "it kind of flattened out a little bit," said the U.S. Postal team's Tyler Hamilton, who had recovered from earlier stomach problems. "I gave it a go. I attacked from the main group of maybe at the time 25 or 30. I was climbing well to make that attack; I thought if maybe I could get a little time there and make it over the top, I'd be able to help out my higher-placed teammates . . . but it didn't work out."

In front, Serrano couldn't follow Massi, Jimenez, and Rinero, who were now three minutes ahead of the Ullrich-Pantani group. Suddenly, to the riders' left, a break in the clouds high above revealed the last series of hairpins, zigzagging steeply up a bare rock face to the windswept summit. At that moment, just inside 6 kilometers from the top, Pantani made his move.

The Pirate pounced on one of the steepest sections. Gripping the hooks of his bars and almost sprinting out of the saddle, he threw his featherweight Bianchi from side to side to make this a single, decisive attack. Only Frenchman Luc Leblanc went along, but not for long. Behind, Ullrich turned to second-place Bobby Julich, his eyes indicating that he wanted help. But the American, despite his pre-race ambition, later said, "I just didn't have it today. I felt totally blocked on the Galibier."

Pantani attacked decisively through the Galibier rainstorm to leave behind his rivals, Ullrich and Julich.

Once clear, cheered on by his fans, and seeming to ignore the harshness of the weather, Pantani became the incredible climbing machine that won the Plateau de Beille stage five days earlier. Every 100 meters, on average, he was gaining three seconds on the Ullrich group and more on the front three, whom he passed one by one in the final kilometer, to crest the Tour's highest summit, 8,677 feet above sea level, in glorious isolation. Jimenez, Rinero, and Massi followed soon after, with Fernando Escartin, Serrano, and Leblanc about a minute back. Up the final steep "staircase," Julich, despite being shocked by the cold, kept calm and led the six-man yellow-jersey group through the rain and wind. They started the descent an enormous 2:40 behind Pantani.

The temperature at this bleak mountaintop was in the mid-40s—which the windchill took down to the low 30s. It would take tremendous courage, resilience, and daring to race the 34 kilometers downhill in conditions that were almost as bad as when the Galibier section was canceled two years before. And it was in these 34 kilometers of hell that the Tour would be won and lost.

The two groups appeared to be evenly matched. In front, Pantani stopped to put on a rain jacket and thick gloves, allowing four men to rejoin him—but not Jimenez, who was totally unprepared for the cold conditions. Behind, Julich, as he tried to put on his red rain jacket, almost fell on one of the first steep switchbacks. He skidded onto the dirt shoulder, and Ullrich rode by him as the American remounted his bike.

On this first part of the long descent, Ullrich had five men with him, six when they caught Leblanc. On reaching the turn onto a wider, less steep road at the Col de Lautaret, the chasers had closed to within 2:11. It looked as if Ullrich was going to save his jersey, especially when six more riders joined his group. But once on the bigger road, descending into a deep valley between towering rock walls, Pantani's group appeared better organized. Massi, a friend of The Pirate, was making long pulls, as were Escartin and his Kelme teammate, Serrano. Only Rinero, defending Julich's position, sat on.

In pursuit, Julich was helping Ullrich, but the German had no teammates to support him. In theory the race's top two time-trialists—Ullrich and Julich—should have been going faster than the four climbers in front. But with more than four hours of racing completed, and three of those hours spent climbing, a rider's capacity is not the same as on a flat stage, particularly in cold, wet weather.

Ullrich seemed more fatigued than his rivals, undoubtedly affected not only by the rigors of the stage but also by the immense pressure on him since he took the yellow jersey in the Corrèze time trial a week before. And unlike the case in 1997, he was the only Telekom rider left in front, Bjarne Riis and Udo Bölts having been dropped halfway up the Galibier.

The visual evidence was confirmed by the time splits taken in the next few minutes: 2:18 at La Grave, the town opposite the grand, glaciated Meije mountain, now hidden by clouds, 25 kilometers from the finish; 2:33 with 20 kilometers to go; 2:47 with 17 kilometers to go. Ullrich seemed to be in a trance, and after drifting to the back of his group to collect a water bottle and raincoat, the next split showed the gap to be 3:14, Pantani had overcome his overall deficit of 3:01 and was now the virtual race leader.

Then, just before crossing a dam to start the final climb to Les Deux-Alpes, Ullrich's hand went up. He had a front-wheel flat, but in his distressed condition he was slow in stopping, and there seemed no urgency in his reactions as a mechanic changed the wheel and team director Walter Godefroot pushed the race leader back into action.

Up the final climb—only 8.5 kilometers long, yet almost a mini–Alpe d'Huez—the three protagonists showed their relative strengths at the end of this terrifying stage.

Pantani immediately dropped his four breakaway companions with a repeat of his Galibier surge. And he never faltered in his triumphant march toward the yellow jersey, leaving Massi and Escartin almost two minutes back by the top. Pantani crossed the line, a smile on his bearded face, in an atmosphere of near-delirium caused by the brilliance of the Italian wonder's stage win, the Wagnerian weather, and the drama of Ullrich's unexpected predicament.

After his puncture, Ullrich did not get back to the chase group before the climb, where Julich immediately attacked. The American's burst split the group,

The sun came out to greet Pantani at Les Deux-Alpes after his epic breakaway to take the Tour's yellow jersey.

and Dutchman Michael Boogerd was the only one to fight back up to him. Even so, Julich said at the finish, "I didn't feel good. I was just trying to limit my losses on Pantani."

Showing his determination, Julich first threw off his rain jacket, then swapped his helmet for a cycling cap, as he and Boogerd passed the 8 kilometers-to-go sign 4:04 behind Pantani, with Ullrich at 4:41. Julich never looked back, virtually ignoring Boogerd, who would slowly drop back. The American battled all the way to the line, matching the pace of Massi and Escartin, to take fifth place, 5:43 down. Full of admiration for his conqueror, Julich said, "Incredible, Pantani. I knew he was very, very dangerous. I didn't know he could do what he did today. He made us all look silly."

Ullrich looked desperate. Everything that had happened since he won the 1997 Tour was catching up with him: the receptions and sponsor photo shoots, the overlong winter break, the overweight spring, and the overblown German media blitzkrieg expecting him to repeat as Tour champion. Although Riis and Bölts were catching back and pacing him up the final hill, Ullrich couldn't go any faster. His losses were growing by the minute. His face was a red mask, his eyes puffy, as rain lashed into him, hiding his tears. The gap was 5:43 with 5 kilometers to go—and that grew to an enormous 8:57 by the finish line.

Falling to fourth overall, Ullrich had lost the yellow tunic to Pantani in as dramatic a fashion as Geminiani had conceded the Tour to Gaul 40 years before. Pantani's old-fashioned attack 48 kilometers from the finish was full of risks, but it was also full of a resilience that few thought him capable of. Ignoring the terrible conditions, he seemed to summon up all his talent and strength to make this "the most beautiful day of my career."

WHEN IT WAS SUGGESTED a few months before the 1998 Tour that Marco Pantani would win the race, most people smiled and snickered under their breath. Why? In his three previous appearances at the world's toughest bike race, Pantani had acquired a reputation as a rider who could win a few mountain stages but who didn't have the speed to contain rivals like Miguel Induráin or Jan Ullrich in 60-kilometer time trials. Furthermore, even if he did take the yellow jersey, few believed that his Mercatone Uno team would have the strength to keep it on his back.

What the naysayers didn't see was the progress Pantani had been making, nor the promise he had shown before the terrible accident he suffered at the Milan-Turin race on October 18, 1995. Prior to that near-fatal collision with an SUV, Pantani had made a pretty good start in the grand tours: He was second at the 1991 Giro d'Italia, third in the 1994 Tour, and after missing the

Whenever Pantani needed help at the 1998 Tour, his Mercatone Uno team was united behind him.

1995 Giro because of a training accident just before the start, he began that year's Tour short of fitness yet came through in the mountains to win stages at L'Alpe d'Huez and Guzet-Neige to take 13th overall.

After missing both the Giro and the Tour in 1996 because of rehab needed for his multiple-fractured left leg, Pantani returned to the big tour scene in 1997. But once again misfortune struck. He crashed while descending a steep hill on the Giro's eighth stage after a cat ran across the road and caused a pileup. A month later at the Tour, short of form again, he was out of contention, seven minutes back, even before reaching the mountains. Nonetheless, Pantani scored two mountain stage wins and climbed up to third place overall by Paris.

In 1998 The Pirate made the Giro his season goal and put everything into winning it. On every stage that had a hill to climb, Pantani attacked. "I didn't give it a second thought," he said. "I put out a lot of energy." Already popular with the *tifosi*, his die-hard cycling fans, Pantani's aggressive riding had them practically willing him to victory in the Dolomites, which he achieved by riding Alex Zülle into oblivion and then breaking defending champion Pavel Tonkov on the mountaintop finish at Montecampione. Significantly, Pantani took the leader's pink jersey after a 50-kilometer breakaway, first alone and then with Italian rival Giuseppe Guerini. And to clinch his overall victory, The Pirate placed third in the last time trial.

But the Giro is not the Tour, people said, and Pantani won in Italy only because there were so many more mountain stages and shorter time trials than he would face in France. Also weighing against Pantani at the Tour, it seemed, was his fatigue from the Giro: He took off ten days and then trained, mostly alone, for the remaining three weeks before the Tour started in Dublin. And when Pantani placed 181st in the prologue time trial, and went on to finish right at the end of the field in each of the first six road stages, everyone wrote him off as a challenger at the Tour. Even Pantani had his doubts. "It's true," he said, looking back. "In the first week, I didn't think I would wear the yellow jersey. But I didn't waste any energy. And in my heart of hearts, there was always this window of opportunity that remained open, so I didn't let the seconds go to my opponents."

While Pantani steadily rode himself into form, not losing time in crashes, he had a wonderfully quiet opening 10 days. Unlike Ullrich, who was always under the media microscope because of his 1997 Tour victory, Pantani wasn't harassed at all. He was often in the team's camper van and on the way to his hotel within 10 minutes of a stage finish. The little Italian—122 pounds and 5-foot-7—continued to be ignored when he placed only 33rd in the 58-kilometer Corrèze time trial, 4:21 behind Ullrich. But after he took second place at Luchon, and then won the stage up to Plateau de

> The objective was to gain seconds without thinking about Ullrich or the others . . . but to stay concentrated. It was my day, the day of my courage and my resistance.

Beille, moving into fourth place overall, only 3:01 down on yellow-jersey Ullrich, the skeptics began saying, without much conviction, "Oh, yeah, maybe Pantani could even win this Tour."

That "window of opportunity" had widened a little, and the Italian wonder climber was ready to make a real bid for victory on the stage to Les Deux-Alpes. "When I started the Galibier stage, I wanted to try to make a big exploit," Pantani said. "And as I gained seconds at every kilometer in my attack on the Galibier, that's what mattered. The objective was to gain seconds without thinking about Ullrich or the others . . . but to stay concentrated. It was my day, the day of my courage and my resistance.

"It was difficult for me to withstand the cold, and in the descent [of the Galibier] it was very cold. I was at the limit of being overcome on the descent.

The Pantani fans were out in force at the 1998 Tour.

Then, on the last climb [to Les Deux-Alpes], I had incredible determination. It was the day when I had the will to put everything together."

His epic breakaway, almost the same length as the one he had made in the Giro over the Marmolada to Selva–Val Gardena, wrote a page that cycling historians will always turn to when legendary rides are remembered. That horrifically wet, cold day in the Alps saw Pantani climb to glory and Ullrich battle to defeat. And finally, the naysayers had to admit they were wrong, that *this* Pantani was someone they hadn't seen developing.

But let the winner of the 1998 Tour de France sum it up in his own words: "Of the four Tours I've done, this was the most difficult. But in saying that— and I don't want to boast—but if there hadn't been Pantani, perhaps no one would have put Jan Ullrich in crisis, and perhaps it would have been the same result as last year. And everyone would have said Jan Ullrich is the strongest. But there was something different in this Tour—perhaps it was a different Pantani, a more mature Pantani, one with more experience, and more training. So I was very happy with the order of the finish."

In this troubled Tour, it was his humble personality and spectacular climbing that made the race vibrate with excitement, just when it threatened to be shaken to its death by the infamous Festina doping scandal. Pantani, who often spoke of himself and his performances in the third person, really did have two distinct personas. There was Marco the man—introspective and thoughtful of others (he kept a picture of his late friend Fabio Casartelli at his bedside)—and Marco the myth—whose marvelous rides created a legend that threatens to make him the world's most popular cyclist since Fausto Coppi. Already a legend in Italy, Pantani was the first Italian since Coppi to take the Tour and Giro in the same season, and the first Italian to win the Tour since Felice Gimondi in 1965. Gimondi, looking as handsome as in his heyday, joined Pantani on the Paris podium in congratulations.

Italy's 1965 Tour winner Felice Gimondi congratulated his successor 33 years later.

Pantani had another hero, Charly Gaul, the Luxembourger who won the Tour in 1958 with his fabulous solo breakaway in the Alps. When the aging Luxembourger and the young Pantani had met the previous winter, they ended up agreeing that the one thing that mattered in cycling, or indeed in life itself, was "man and his courage." In the end, Pantani, his last-day bleached yellow beard adding to his swashbuckling image, beat Ullrich by 3:21, while Julich completed the podium another 47 seconds back. The Pirate had finally found his treasure.

Expulsion
from the Giro

"I'M EMBITTERED. MORE THAN ANYTHING, I'm sorry for the fans." Marco's eyes are swollen. He exits the main door of the three-star Hotel Touring and faces the television cameras, demonstrating a certain confidence. "Many things could be said, but they would only be additional words. If things like this happen to me, an athlete who has given a lot to the sport of cycling, it's cause for reflection. I had already been tested twice; I already had the *maglia rosa,* and my hematocrit level was 46 percent. But now I awake to this surprise; something strange is going on."

Marco's face is so dark that he seems even skinnier than usual. He is wearing a gray post-race T-shirt; the pink jersey is back on the floor of his room. "After an experience like this, I need to make some decisions, even if reluctantly," he says. "I've had to start over after terrible accidents, but this time I'm emotionally shattered. This time I've hit rock bottom."

A question rises from the forest of microphones: "So, you're quitting cycling?"

"I already said so," is his laconic response. After a moment of dead silence, Pantani continues, "Now I just want a little respect. I'd like to say hi to my fans. I'm sorry for the sport of cycling, which comes out of this looking bad."

Andrea Agostini, Pantani's friend and spokesperson, steps in and leads him away. It's 1:05 P.M. Marco climbs into the Citroën station wagon his sports director, Giuseppe Martinelli, is driving. The car is surrounded by dozens of fans applauding him. His Mercatone Uno–Bianchi teammates, Ermanno Brignoli, Marco Velo, Massimo Podenzana, and Simone Borgheresi, are following the scene from a balcony and wave to their captain who is leaving the Giro.

The rider from Romagna was encamped in his hotel room for more than four hours. His blood test at 7:30 A.M. seemed like a formality. After breakfast, Pantani went back to his room to get ready, while Martinelli went to a nearby hotel to get the test results. By 10 A.M., it was already clear what was happening. Outside the team's hotel, the mechanics had prepared the bikes as they

"I just want a little respect," Pantani said as he left the 1999 Giro under a cloud of suspicion.

always did. But only eight were lined up against the wall. Marco Pantani's black bike bearing the No. 1 race number was missing. The long faces of Alessandro Giannelli, Martinelli's assistant director, and the *soigneur*, Roberto Pregnolato, said more than any words could convey.

At 10:12 A.M., the official announcement was delivered: Marco Pantani has been declared unfit for competition. Martinelli returns from the blood inspectors' hotel and goes to see Pantani right away. "Yes, I was the one who shared the news with him," explains the director of Mercatone Uno–Bianchi. "His head was hanging, and he didn't move an inch."

> "Marco will go home and saw his bike in half," she says. "If I know him well at all, we won't see him on a bike again."

Those who were in the room describe scenes of immense anguish. Martinelli lying on the bed, weeping openly. Pantani, outraged, puts his fist through the window. Papà Ferdinando remaining motionless without saying a word. "I want nothing more to do with cycling or bikes. What they've done to me is too much," Pantani is reported to have said. His friend Agostini, who accompanied him during the entire Giro, is disillusioned. "Marco will go home and saw his bike in half," she says. "If I know him well at all, we won't see him on a bike again."

The situation gets worse. At 10:15 A.M., Zaina and Velo come down from their rooms to speak on behalf of the team. "Without Marco, we're not going anywhere. We all stand by him." The word gets out to the caravan, and the hotel is inundated with journalists, friends, and the curious. Two four-person teams of *carabinieri*, the peak-capped Italian police, are deployed in the name of public order to keep the peace.

Pantani leaves the hotel at 1:05 P.M. After the team captain leaves, so does the rest of the squad. Ten minutes later, only a trail of bitterness remains.

Marco arrives in Imola to undergo further blood tests in a UCI-accredited laboratory. In the two tests, his hematocrit levels measure at 47.6 and 48.1 percent. In the emergency room at Imola, Pantani has his right hand tended to, the one he used to punch through the hotel window. That evening, first at the stage village and then at the hotel that accommodated the panel of judges, three *carabinieri* show up with a warrant for confiscation of documentation: They are looking for the records declaring the panel's verdict that the cyclist in question was unfit to participate in the sport of cycling. The documents are produced by the panel's president, Joseph Bochaca. At 7:20 P.M., Saturday night, Marco Pantani arrives at his residence in Cesenatico. The following day, the Giro will finish in Milan. Without this blood problem, Marco would be there, wearing the *maglia rosa*, celebrating his second Giro victory in two years. Instead he's all alone. It will be almost nine months before he starts another race.

"Anger in My Heart"

THE SYMBOLISM WAS IMPOSSIBLE TO IGNORE. At the Vatican in Rome on May 13, 2000, after a tumultuous and scandal-filled year, Marco Pantani returned to competitive cycling where he had left it: at the Giro d'Italia. He had made a halting attempt at racing in February, so there were doubts if he, the winner of both the 1998 Tour de France and the Giro, would even make it to the starting line in Rome. Indeed, for Pantani it must have seemed a long, long way from the time two years earlier when he was universally hailed as the savior of cycling, one of the few people capable of guiding the Tour de France through its darkest hours.

Throughout the infamous Festina scandal at the 1998 Tour de France, Pantani had stayed focused on the race. As teams and riders were ejected, arrested, or withdrew from the Tour in protest, Pantani remained a solid figure, concentrating on the challenges at hand and reminding those around him that the race itself was something that needed to be protected, respected, and preserved. As prosecutors filed charges against the team directors of Festina and TVM, Pantani helped steer the 1998 Tour toward its conclusion in Paris—something that had been in doubt soon after police stopped *soigneur* Willy Voet's Festina team car and discovered more than 400 vials of the blood-boosting

During his series of runaway stage wins at the 1999 Giro, neither The Pirate nor the Devil could have foreseen that Pantani would be skewered before the end.

drug EPO, a human growth hormone and an assortment of other performance-enhancing substances. At least Pantani's performance, many suggested, could allay the fears and cynicism swirling around the sport. The little Italian climbing sensation was proof that the cycling sport could be saved by someone who didn't need a sophisticated and organized doping program to succeed. It was an illusion that was placed in doubt less than a year later, just as Pantani was poised to win the 1999 Giro.

HIS EJECTION FROM THE GIRO at Madonna di Campiglio began a year that would eventually see Pantani publicly shamed, investigated, and ultimately indicted by prosecutors. The sport and its governing body were shaken. UCI President Hein Verbruggen expressed disappointment that the rider upon whom many had staked their hopes was now at the center of his own controversy. "It's not only traumatic for the Giro, but also for cycling," he said, not mentioning the trauma the cyclist himself was going through.

In his defense, Pantani strenuously denied any involvement with doping. The test he "failed" was not regarded as definitive proof that he had used EPO, the commercially produced recombinant form of the human hormone erythropoietin. At the time, no acceptable test to detect the drug existed. Instead the UCI did its best to guard against its abuse by testing for the effects of the drug. The hormone is naturally produced by the kidney in the event of hypoxia—the point at which the body signals that its muscles are not receiving enough oxygen. Increased levels of erythropoietin in the blood

> "It's not only traumatic for the Giro, but also for cycling," said UCI President Hein Verbruggen.

95

trigger receptors and prompt the bone marrow to produce more red blood cells. It is an elegant and beautifully subtle system constantly monitored by a healthy human body.

For patients suffering from chronic anemia, either from kidney failure or some external cause like chemotherapy, EPO is a wonder drug. It can raise a dangerously low red-blood-cell count—below 28 or 29 percent—to a healthy level of 39 to 43 percent. Patients, once too exhausted to climb out of bed in the morning, can now lead close to normal lives.

Upon EPO's commercial release in the late 1980s, unscrupulous doctors and athletes have seen its performance potential in raising a healthy hematocrit of, say, 43 percent to 50, 55, 60, or even higher. That more-is-better philosophy is believed by some to have been the cause of a spate of mysterious deaths among cyclists in the late 1980s and early 1990s. It is also what prompted the UCI to impose an upper hematocrit limit of 50 percent in 1996. With rare exception granted to those who could prove a naturally higher-than-normal red-blood-cell count, the UCI began imposing a mandatory two-week "rest period" on anyone found to exceed 50 percent. The short penalty and euphemistic language were intended to skirt the inevitable legal challenges resulting from efforts to control the use of a drug for which there was no effective test.

But in Pantani's case, the penalty was significantly longer than the mandated rest period of two weeks. Theoretically, Pantani could have returned to racing at the 1999 Tour de France and defended his title. He did not. Nor did he compete for the remainder of the year. He variously explained his absence as having both emotional and physical causes, and did not directly address the allegations of drug use that surrounded him.

By November 1999, prosecutors in Turin, florence, and Forli decided it was time to raise the stakes and force Pantani to talk.

The press release issued by the Mercatone Uno team was brief: "Marco Pantani has been summoned by the Turin state prosecutor, as someone under investigation, for Thursday, November 11 at 10 A.M."

It was to be his second summons in as many weeks. A week earlier, Pantani had already been quizzed for three hours by antidrug police in Florence, part of an inquiry into doping by Ferrara prosecutor Guido Soprani. Michele Leoni, the state prosecutor in the northern city of Forli, was also opening an investigation.

As for the meeting in Turin, team director Giuseppe Martinelli said he didn't know what to expect. "At the moment, I just don't know what to say, and I can't judge the actions of the magistrates who have summoned Marco Pantani."

State prosecutor Raffaele Guariniello was pursuing the matter under the provisions of a 1989 law that allowed anyone "tampering with the outcome of a sporting event" to be charged with a crime. Though intended as a means of prosecuting gamblers trying to "fix" an event, the law was interpreted by some as allowing the prosecution of athletes who derived some sort of competitive advantage by using a performance-enhancing drug. Logic and the appeals system upheld that interpretation. It was a charge that could carry a jail sentence ranging from three months to two years and fines ranging from 5 million ($3,000) to 50 million lira ($30,000).

That Thursday morning, Pantani did appear as ordered at the office of state prosecutor Guariniello. Accompanied by his manager, Manuela Ronchi, Pantani entered the office for what was expected to be a one- to two-hour session. He emerged minutes later announcing that he had exercised his right to silence. "I reject the accusation and am exercising my right not to answer questions," he told Guariniello.

Pantani suggested that the blood test at the Giro and the subsequent investigations were merely an attempt to ruin his career and sully his reputation among the *tifosi*. "I feel that they are much closer to me than certain people would like," he said as he left Guariniello's office.

While the 1999 Giro was the event that triggered the investigation, Guariniello appeared to be most interested in an incident that took place long before that: the 1995 Milan-Turin accident that shattered Pantani's leg and threatened to end his promising career. Indeed, the injury and his subsequent recovery and comeback were used as indicators of the feisty Italian's heroism. Now, Guariniello (along with Leoni in Forli) was examining the event as an indicator of Pantani's willingness to cheat.

An initial review of emergency room medical records from the Turin hospital where his broken leg was treated showed that Pantani had exhibited an

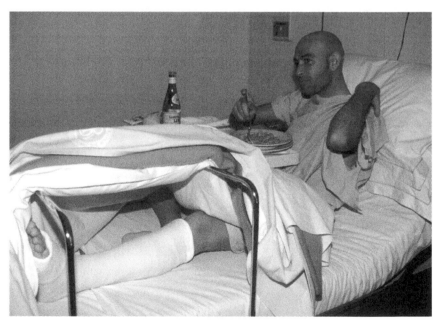

A blood test taken after Pantani's left leg was broken in a 1995 crash showed an astoundingly high red-blood-cell count.

astoundingly high red-blood-cell count. Blood tests at the time showed a hematocrit level between 59.3 and 61 percent. The level was well beyond natural and would be in keeping with what was assumed to be common among cheating cyclists a year before the UCI began regular hematocrit testing.

Guariniello was also interested in the mysterious disappearance of blood samples taken by doctors at a hospital near Salerno after an accident involving Pantani during the 1997 Giro. The possible offense in that investigation, he said, would be "falsification by removal" of evidence.

Pantani and his attorneys seemed taken aback by the investigation's shift in focus. In his defense, Pantani argued that during competition, particularly after a 200-kilometer race that ended in a car crash, "any athlete's blood count is subject to change." It was an argument he also raised regarding the test taken at the 1999 Giro. "After training at altitude, days spent racing in the mountains, and dehydration, it is perfectly normal to see a rise in hematocrit," his doctor, Roberto Rempi, was quoted as saying.

A MEDICAL DEFENSE MAY NOT have been Pantani's best option. As for his assertion that the 1999 and 1995 results were within normal parameters, medical experts enlisted by the prosecutor's office in Forli disputed that.

Biologists examined the 1995 samples and concluded that "the exogenous assumption of erythropoietin, which has a half-life of around six hours, could explain virtually all of the biological parameters that appear to have changed in the blood sample provided by Marco Pantani."

As an example, the experts' report, issued in February 2000, cited iron levels in Pantani's blood that were nearly five times higher than the upper limit of what might be considered normal. Adult males usually have iron levels that vary from 25 to 225 nanograms per milliliter of blood. The samples pulled during the 1999 Giro showed Pantani's count was nearly 1,200 nanograms. Elevated iron levels are among a group of indicators that suggest—though not prove—use of artificial erythropoietin.

The report concluded there was a slight possibility that Pantani had not used the drug. It cautiously noted that it would require "physio-pathological mechanisms . . . hitherto unknown to the scientific world" to otherwise explain the results.

DESPITE THE EMBARRASSMENT of the report and the likelihood of impending prosecution, Pantani tried to bring his focus back to racing. He marked his return to the professional peloton during February's Tour of Valencia in Spain. It was a difficult and halting beginning, and a frustrated Pantani pulled out during the third stage.

He then set his sights on another Spanish race, the Tour of Murcia, but didn't show up. Meanwhile, Rempi, the Mercatone Uno team doctor at the 1999 Giro, was indicted in Trento on charges of "manipulating the results of sporting events" by providing his riders—Pantani in particular—with performance-enhancing drugs. Pantani was shaken and announced that he was putting his cycling career on hold. He wrote an open letter to team director Martinelli explaining his reasons: "I want to return to cycling with sincerity and enthusiasm. At the moment, even if from a physical point of view I am able to race, I am going through a difficult period involving much internal suffering. I need a rest, and as things stand I can't say for how long."

Then, in April 2000, Leoni, the state prosecutor in Forli, indicted Pantani under the same 1989 law that Rempi was charged with violating.

As the Giro d'Italia approached, speculation was running rampant throughout Italy that Pantani would stage a dramatic return. He was rumored to be training. Reports filtered back that he had been seen climbing on some of the very roads over which this Giro would be fought. Among the *tifosi*, the excitement was tangible.

On May 4, just nine days before the start of the Giro in Rome, Pantani's name appeared on the start list submitted by Mercatone Uno. "A sign of someone else's wishful thinking," said Pantani, denying reports that he would be at the race. He was in Ferrara to present evidence in yet another doping case when he said that he *might* compete at the Tour de France in July.

... just nine days before the start of the Giro in Rome, Pantani's name appeared on the start list submitted by Mercatone Uno. "A sign of someone else's wishful thinking," said Pantani, denying reports that he would be at the race.

"I don't know when I'll return to racing," he said, "but it'll be when I'm in just the right state of mind. I hope that won't be long. But I'm not making any promises, because it would be sad if I couldn't keep them. I'm doing what I can to get back my peace of mind and to make my comeback. I've always kept up my training, even though I haven't been able to do much because so many other things have interfered. . . . But I've never abandoned my profession."

The excitement tapered, but the *tifosi* remained hopeful. And this time their hopes were fulfilled. The night before the start of the Giro, Mercatone Uno–Bianchi president Felice Gimondi confirmed that "The Pirate is back" and would be competing the next day in Rome.

Gimondi made the announcement as participants, including Pantani, arrived at the Vatican for a private audience with Pope John Paul II. What better setting to start one's journey to redemption?

PANTANI IMMEDIATELY BEGAN TO minimize expectations for his performance in the Giro. "I am here to ride in support of my team. I am here to regain my form." Indeed, it was the Giro's eventual winner, Stefano Garzelli—once known as the "little Pirate"—and not Pantani who was designated as Mercatone Uno's team leader. Pantani insisted he was racing to support his once-tireless lieutenant.

"But, ahh, when the mountains come . . ." seemed to be the mantra of the die-hard fans lining the roads. Italian television cameras focused much of their attention on Pantani. News from the road included status reports on the day's stage leader and his position relative to that of the group that contained the overall leader *"Gruppo maglia rosa"* and, a relatively new subject of interest, the *"Gruppo Pantani."*

Pantani's performance on the Giro's first climb above 1,000 meters (3,280 feet) in stage 3 was thoroughly analyzed and dutifully reported to waiting Italian television audiences. But the real anticipation was focused on stage 9's ascent of San Pellegrino in Alpe, a climb that averaged almost 9 percent for 12.6 kilometers. This, said the *tifosi,* was where *Il Pirata* would make his move. No, it was where a rival, Francesco Casagrande, made *his* move.

Casagrande took charge of the Giro right where he predicted he would: on the slopes of the San Pellegrino. The 1988 Giro winner, Andy Hampsten, had traveled to the climb from his home in Tuscany that day. The crowds, he noted, were filled with anticipation of a stellar performance by Pantani, their favorite rider. "There must have been all of Tuscany and half of the northern tribes there to watch Pantani sail away," Hampsten later wrote. "You could have heard a pin drop when he didn't."

Pantani crawled over the summit some seven minutes after Casagrande. It was a pattern he would repeat as the Giro moved to the northern mountains, losing 17:32 on stage 13's brutal ride from Feltre to Selva Gardena, and losing still more time the next day as the Giro crossed the infamous Passo di Gavia.

The fans had come to the realization that Pantani would not be making a dramatic comeback. They could only hope for one significant performance—an indication, perhaps, of things to come. It finally came on stage 19, through the Alps to Briançon, France, coincidentally the site of a scheduled stage finish for the 2000 Tour de France as well.

NEARLY AN HOUR BEHIND in the overall standings, it was clear that Pantani could do little in this Giro except show that he still had the aggressive style and remarkable climbing form that had once characterized his career. That day's stage over the highest point in the Giro, the Colle dell Agnello, and then the famed Col d'Izoard, was perfect for showing that the old Pantani was still there. The 15-kilometer Agnello, like the Gavia, is made up of a series of narrow switchbacks that reach grades of 13 percent.

Throughout the day, race leader Casagrande seemed content to shadow his main rivals, Garzelli and a brash 28-year-old Italian, Gilberto Simoni. Simoni was not content to simply stay with the *maglia rosa*. On the Agnello he charged off the front repeatedly, finally managing to get some distance, with only Paolo Lanfranchi in his company. By the summit, Simoni and Lanfranchi were close to catching an earlier break. Behind them in close pursuit were

Fans had to wait until stage 19 of the Giro to see the "old" Pantani as he helped teammate Garzelli (left) prepare his bid for overall victory.

Casagrande, Garzelli, and others. It was turning into a dramatic stage. But the Italian fans lining the Agnello were focusing their attention on the man in close pursuit of Casagrande. They were cheering wildly, not because of the drama at the front but because their hero, Pantani, was finally making a show of it. There he was flashing the same style, the same panache, he had displayed through most of the 1999 Giro.

All the problems of the previous year, all the disappointment of this Giro, all the frustration, and all the embarrassment suddenly disappeared as Pantani crested the Agnello in hot pursuit of the leaders. The Pirate was back. Toward the top of the Izoard, and to the thrill of the *tifosi*, Pantani was with the leaders. Presumably he was there to lend support to his teammate Garzelli. Indeed, Italian television replayed and replayed again the moment when Pantani handed his teammate a water bottle. It was a role they were unaccustomed to seeing and one Pantani was apparently unaccustomed to playing.

Pantani attacked and attacked, occasionally leaving Garzelli behind and unwittingly towing Simoni along with him. Behind them, Lanfranchi had retreated to help his team leader, Pavel Tonkov, over the top of the Izoard. The pair chased and eventually bridged up to the leaders. Just as they rejoined, Lanfranchi charged ahead. "It hadn't been my plan to attack," Lanfranchi later explained, "but with everyone else watching each other, it was time for me to try something."

Lanfranchi quickly built up a one-minute lead. Behind him, Pantani charged off the front of the chase group, leaving his own teammate, Garzelli, behind. Lanfranchi realized he had the win and celebrated as he crossed the line. Pantani rode alone through an adoring mob as Simoni, Garzelli, and Casagrande chased him. He would later explain that day's performance as a response to a year of frustration, disappointment, and above all, anger. "I did not ride this way today because of the strength in my legs," he said in a post-race press conference. "I rode like this because of the anger in my heart. I wanted to make a statement."

Garzelli, who moved into the overall lead the next day, would later credit Pantani for "an inspiring performance" into Briançon. His teammate, he said, was instrumental in convincing him that he could win the Giro. Still, though Garzelli dedicated his win to his teammate, he knew that eventually he would be back in the role of lieutenant. By the fall of 2000, Garzelli would begin looking for a place on another team.

Pantani, meanwhile, ignored the indictments, ignored the legal problems, forgot the troubled spring, and turned his attention toward the 2000 Tour de France.

Duel on the Ventoux

MONT VENTOUX, FRANCE *July 13, 2000*

ITS PRESENCE WAS FELT by the riders during their training rides on the first rest day of the 2000 Tour de France. They saw it floating in the distance like a white saddleback whale on a sea of green vineyards. They had heard talk about it on television: the mythical mountain where Tom Simpson died in 1967 and champions Charly Gaul and Eddy Merckx took stage wins on their way to victories in the Tours of 1958 and 1970, respectively. They had seen its details in the race bible: 21 kilometers of climbing at 7.6 percent, an elevation gain of 5,249 feet, and the steepest pitches of 13, 14, and 15 percent. And now it had arrived: the race to the top of Mont Ventoux.

> They saw it floating in the distance like a white saddleback whale on a sea of green vineyards.

Though this relatively short stage of 149 kilometers started in Carpentras, only 15 kilometers from the mountain's base, it seemed to take forever to reach it. The organizers had laid out a complicated course, first heading away from the Ventoux before taking a circuitous loop across the windswept plains and along the roller-coaster backroads of Provence.

The first distant view of the giant peak came from a small ridge 20 kilometers into the stage, where the field had just come together after an intense bout of racing, pushed by a three-quarter tailwind. The next clear view of the mountain came from a narrow road climbing away from the pocket-sized vineyards toward a thin forest of cork oak trees at 29 kilometers, where the day's first attacks were forming and a dozen riders were chasing back through the team cars after a pile-up.

Then, heading toward an exquisitely beautiful valley of purple and gold fields, was the first close-up view of the mountain across lines of aromatic lavender and burnished wheat. Here a nine-man break had formed on the fast, sinuous downhill from the Col de Murs and was in the process of taking a 4:50 lead over the peloton.

That gap didn't please the Banesto team *directeur sportif* Eusebio Unzue, who was planning a stage win by his climber José Maria Jimenez. The injection of pace from Banesto, helped by a gusting wind, started on the first, wide-open slopes of the day's third climb. And over the plateau-like summit, down the long, swooping, into-the-wind descent, and along a twisting country road through the Vaucluse vineyards, the gap fell by three minutes. So the break began climbing the first easy slopes of the Ventoux only 1:35 ahead of the pack instead of five minutes or more.

Five kilometers into the climb, where the narrow road turned left away from the grapevines and into a tight, pine-clad limestone hollow, the grade suddenly zoomed from 3 to 9 percent. Within a kilometer, Santiago Botero and Alex Vinokourov rode away from the break, and the U.S. Postal team's Tyler Hamilton took over from Banesto at the head of the pack. The American, who had won the stage to the Ventoux summit in the Dauphiné Libéré a month

Lance Armstrong (left) and Pantani battled 70-kph winds to the summit of Mont Ventoux at the 2000 Tour.

earlier, went so fast that only a handful of riders could hold his wheel. Among those dropped, ironically, was Jimenez.

By the time Hamilton had finished his impressive stint for his team leader Lance Armstrong and their teammate Kevin Livingston had taken over, Botero and Vinokourov had been caught, while the only men left with Armstrong and Livingston were Jan Ullrich, Roberto Heras, Joseba Beloki, and Pantani. "Pantani was just coming off the group when I dropped off," Hamilton later said.

Heras then put in a probing attack, which caused Vinokourov and Livingston to be dropped, and saw Pantani lose about 25 meters. But Pantani was receiving huge support from the fans packed solidly on both sides of the road, and he set about catching back up. It was a difficult task. From 100 meters back, he was simply matching the pace set by the steady Ullrich, who was now leading the break.

The grade, too, became more even on the long stretch before the famous left turn at Chalet Reynard, 6.5 kilometers from the top. This long, curving bend—where perhaps 10,000 of the Ventoux's estimated 300,000 spectators were watching from a natural amphitheater—took the leaders away from the shelter of the trees and out into the wind howling across the bare, scree-like ridge. It felt more like Everest than like the Ventoux.

Almost immediately, the pace slowed, and Pantani came back up to the lead group, the strongest seven men in the race. Frenchman Richard Virenque was the first to attack, but he was easily countered. Then, 5.5 kilometers from the summit, Pantani put in the first of what would prove to be a whole series of accelerations. The third of these saw Virenque drop back, and the fourth was answered only by Botero. Together, the Italian and Colombian moved 11 seconds ahead. Pantani surged again, dropping Botero, and at the same time Armstrong finally made the charge everyone was expecting. The man in the yellow jersey rose out of the saddle, virtually sprinting, and went quickly past Botero before joining Pantani with about 3 kilometers still to go.

If things unfolded the same as they had at Hautacam, three days earlier, Armstrong's next surge would take him solo. But Pantani later said he was now feeling better than he did in the Pyrenees, "although it's not the real Pantani." Real or not, the shaven-headed one was making a good impersonation of Pantani '98, and he pulled back onto Armstrong's wheel. They briefly spoke and settled into sharing a steadier tempo—although the Texan was doing the stronger pulls—until, with a kilometer to go, they led the chasing Ullrich and Beloki by 30 seconds.

That gap pretty much stayed the same as the two leaders and two chasers all struggled against the fierce wind, gusting to 70 kilometers per hour, on the last 10 percent pitch. The rider in yellow and his rival in pink then made the steep right turn toward the finish line. Everyone expected a final duel between the two men who had conquered the Giant of Provence. But, anticlimactically, Armstrong didn't contest the sprint and a gasping Pantani crossed a finish line as a winner for the first time since he left the 1999 Giro d'Italia in disgrace.

Why did Armstrong give up his chance of winning the stage? "I thought it was the right thing to do, the classy thing to do," the race leader said later. "I like Pantani, and I respect him. And I know the last 12 months have been tough for him."

And now Pantani was back . . . even if it wasn't the "real" Pantani.

The Last
Big Victory

COURCHEVEL, FRANCE *July 16, 2000*

"WHEN YOU DROP EVERYONE, AND finish solo, the victory tastes more like triumph. Yes, this was a victory à la Pantani." One can see the happiness in Pantani's eyes, even though *Il Pirata* is holding it back. Everyone around him is crying: his companion Christina, Manuela Ronchi, Roby Pregnolato, and Beppe Martinelli. Every one of them has a good reason to be crying tears of joy. Marco is in the midst of them with a blank stare, not so much as a grin. But his eyes! Those eyes say it all.

Marco climbs onto the stage to receive flowers and kisses from the podium girls, while the replay of his shaved scalp, open mouth, and devilish glare is shown on the giant screen. Marco, The Pirate, shakes hands, caresses a baby's head, says hello to five-time Tour de France winner Bernard Hinault, now in charge of protocol at the Tour, and receives endless well-wishes from the Tour's race director, Jean-Marie Leblanc. Pantani does it all with a melancholy smile that characterizes his personality, while he always seems engrossed in his thoughts.

Three days after the Ventoux stage win, the "real" Pantani raced to a solo victory at Courchevel.

But as soon as he descends the steps from the stage, it's back to reality. The full court press for interviews begins. "The victory on Ventoux," he explains, "was the first after a rough year and it took place at a prestigious finish, but this one has a sweeter taste. Here, I also dropped Armstrong. I wanted to stick it to Lance, because I hadn't stomached the breakaway he dished out the other day on the Izoard. I wouldn't have been happy going home from the Tour without having succeeded in dropping the American."

The relationship between *Il Pirata* and the Texas cowboy is still positive, but the rivalry has grown to the point of transforming itself into competitive aggression. "I have a lot of respect for Lance, and I'm not just saying that, because I'm not used to saying that kind of thing," says Marco. "He is surely the strongest rider in this Tour and deserves to win it. But I hadn't been able to swallow the fact that he was able to ride away from me in the mountains. There was something about it that bothered me. I wanted to see what this guy's true limits were in the mountains. Now I've set things straight."

> "I wanted to stick it to Lance, because I hadn't stomached the breakaway he dished out the other day on the Izoard. I wouldn't have been happy going home from the Tour without having succeeded in dropping the American."

Along the climb and at the finish, one could see many fans waving Italian flags and many tears for this latest achievement. "Those who are now crying for joy are the same people who a year ago were crying out of anger because of my exclusion from the Giro," says Pantani. "They know what I've been through. They're aware of the suffering I've gone through. I have spent long months of reflection, and I got to the point where I wanted to give up and leave this sport. Then one day something clicked, and I went to the Giro looking forward to the Tour.

"I wanted to prove that Pantani is clean, that he is still capable of being the strongest in the mountains. My victory on Ventoux was for me alone, but I want to dedicate this one to Tonina. That's right, to Mamma Tonina, because, like me, she has suffered a lot over these past months."

Now one wonders whether the new Pantani can become even stronger than the old *Il Pirata*. "I'm not yet as stellar as I'd like to be, but on the last part of the climb I was really riding strong," he says. "I was finally able to launch an attack like I used to. Age and experience have made me mentally and physically tougher. I believe I've become stronger in character, but I don't know how much better I can still become physically."

Thanks to this victory at Courchevel, the eighth stage win in his five Tours, Pantani has climbed back into sixth place overall, 9:03 behind the yellow jersey and 1:35 away from the podium. "My goal is to make a profound and positive impression to honor the team and my teammates who are sacrificing for me," he concludes. "You always think about being on the podium, but I think that's out of reach because there are riders ahead of me who are really good at time trialing. More importantly, now I know that I can come back next year to win."

The
Missing Months

MARCO PANTANI'S LONG BUT INEXORABLE journey toward death really began at Madonna di Campiglio on June 5, 1999, that black day when his Giro d'Italia pink jersey was tarnished with blood. Two days before the finish, an above-the-legal-limit hematocrit reading caused his exclusion from a race that he looked assured of winning. "Starting from that day, nothing was the same as before in Marco's life," said Damiano Zoffoli, the mayor of Cesenatico, at Pantani's hometown.

Temperamental and inordinately paranoid, Pantani took himself slowly but surely into a tunnel of depression, a dark sunshine that destroys without leaving a trace. His manager at Bianchi, Felice Gimondi, attempted to bring calmness back into his life, but in vain.

"Marco was destroyed by Madonna di Campiglio," explained Michel Mengozzi, a close friend who tried to help Pantani in the final months of his life. "They dragged out his death over three years. They should have killed him the day after it happened. He was the victim of injustices, and he didn't need seven prosecutors' offices pursuing him."

In June 2003, eight months before his death, Pantani showed signs of his former self on the steepest climbs of the Giro.

The Armstrong-Pantani duel on Mont Ventoux at the 2000 Tour.

Two days before the finish of his final race, the 2003 Giro, Pantani's attack on the climb to Cascate de Toce elicited a response from race leader Gilberto Simoni.

Riding through rain and snow, Pantani couldn't stay with the leaders on the 2003 Giro's Sampeyre climb.

Happier days (right): Marco with his Danish girlfriend, Christina Jonsson, on the marina in his hometown of Cesenatico.

In the spring of his final year of life, Marco Pantani still had his sights set on one last tilt at the Giro and Tour.

(Previous page) The final journey alongside Leonardo's port canal in Cesenatico.

Even the cycling authorities pursued him, including the Italian cycling federation, which suspended him in June 2002 for his suspected use of insulin. An empty syringe with traces of insulin was discovered in his hotel room during the 2001 Giro, a race he did not finish. Even so, only a month after ending the suspension and eight months before he died, Marco Pantani made one last bid to return to the top. He finished 14th at the 2003 Giro, where he distinguished himself on one of the toughest climbs, the Zoncolan. "I'm more peaceful now," he told the reporters. But bad news was about to arrive. His invitation to the Tour de France never came. "Marco dreamed of a revenge against Lance Armstrong, and he was intensely disappointed," revealed a friend who requested anonymity.

Pantani never again suited up for a race. He felt more alone every day. He returned to his mansion in Cesenatico and tried to reestablish contact with Christina Jonsson, his former Danish fiancée, the only woman he truly loved. But she had already moved on.

For a long time Christina accepted Marco's excesses, his whims, and his complex character. Shortly after Pantani's death she said, "I will always love him." They met at a disco in the mid-1990s. "*Buona sera*, I'm Marco Pantani," he said as an introduction. But she hadn't heard of him. He was immediately taken with this young woman who danced at a nightclub to pay her way through art school at Ravenna. She liked him for what he was, not who he was.

Christina agreed to help Marco's parents run their flatbread stand in Cesenatico during the tourist season. She even weathered the storm of sarcasm that came from Mamma Tonina, who said things like "The customer asked for a beer and a coffee, not a smile."

Christina would have liked to have married Marco and given him some children. But Pantani continued to go out on the town with his buddies and return home late. She forgave him—until the day she gave him an ultimatum:

"Marco, cycling is not the only thing in life; think about the people who really love you."

Influenced by his family, who considered this girlfriend too emancipated, too showy, too unstable, Marco left her. He regretted it. The day after the 2003 Giro, which he had finished in the shadow of anonymity, he phoned her. Too late. Christina had rebuilt her life, even though she missed him terribly.

The love affair, like many others, played a fundamental role in Pantani's death. From the window of the hotel room where he died he could see Bagni 61, the beach where he had kissed Christina for the very first time. He probably remembered that embrace as life flashed before him in his infinite distress.

CHRISTINA'S REFUSAL PLUNGED HIM into depression. He took refuge with Michel Mengozzi, the friend who owned a disco in the beach town of Milano Marittima. Pantani stayed at Mengozzi's inn, a big country house protected by three guard dogs, at Predappio in the foothills of the Apennines. Michel was one of the few people who didn't exploit Pantani. "I feel at peace here," Marco said. He put on weight, about 40 pounds. "I have a neck like a bull, eh?" he joked on seeing childhood friend Mario Pugliese. His body was no longer that of an athlete.

Marco passed the time by hunting wild boar with Michel and fishing, apparently at peace, but already a long way from the world of professional cycling. Even so, from time to time he went out on a mountain bike, but with no conviction, no passion.

One day, he suddenly left Predappio, one of those unpredictable decisions for which only he knew the reason. He disappeared. Nobody knew where he was. He didn't return calls to his cell phone. One night, he was found semiconscious on a bench in a seaside resort on the Adriatic. It was serious. His close friends decided to check him into a psychiatric clinic for celebrities at Teolo, in the hills above Padua. He remained there for several days, but when he checked out, he was in danger again, faced by his worst enemy, himself.

In September, three months after the Giro, he appeared in Milan, at the home of his friend and former agent Manuela Ronchi, who had just had a baby boy, Filippo. He vanished again, and the brief reports from people who bumped into him were alarming: Pantani is not doing well;

> One day, he suddenly left Predappio. One of those unpredictable decisions for which only he knew the reason. He disappeared. Nobody knew where he was.

he's having problems; he must be helped. In October, his cycling sponsor, Mercatone Uno, announced that the team would be fully funded in 2004 only if Pantani agreed to lead it. There was no response from Marco, who wasn't feeling at ease anywhere.

In November he made a first trip to Cuba with Mengozzi. There he met Argentine soccer legend Diego Maradona, also a sportsman with a drug problem. The two men decided to meet again soon in Italy. On his return home, Marco promised Italian racer Giovanni Lombardi that he'd start training with him in Argentina.

But there was no follow-up. Marco returned to Cuba, this time alone, and he stayed at an apartment in Havana rented for him by a friend, Lydia. He ate almost exclusively papayas, used the phone all the time, and swallowed fistfuls of pills, antidepressants. He gave the bike he took with him to a child, having never ridden it during his trip, and then went back to join a group of "friends" who did not really wish him well.

There was a rumor that the Italian ambassador phoned Pantani's parents to ask them to come to Cuba and take their son back to Italy because of some potential legal problems. Marco stayed with his family over the Christmas holidays. He promised his father that he would race his bike again in 2004—one more promise that wouldn't be honored.

The infernal spiral continued to suck Pantani downward. On January 13, 2004, Mengozzi tried to give his friend some fun by organizing a party at his disco for a few friends to celebrate Marco's birthday. The dinner ended in a scuffle. Pantani even took issue with his true friends, the diehards who only wanted to lend a hand. "I don't know who to have confidence in anymore," he said to them in a menacing tone. "I don't know who is with me out of pure friendship or who has ulterior motives." He then calmed down. But some of them said he didn't speak anymore that evening.

The countdown was accelerating. Sergio Neri, director of *BiciSport* magazine, tried to come to Pantani's aid, in secret, with help from Mario Cipollini. The idea was as follows: Persuade Marco to go and get treatment for his drug addiction with the Encounter Community, an organization founded by Italian priest Don Gelmini, which has one of its centers on a 10,000-acre estate in Bolivia, far away from the world that was destroying Marco.

He was scheduled to leave for Bolivia on February 27. But other problems came up. Pantani no longer had control of his possessions. The family was afraid he'd squander his savings, so Papà Pantani took over the management of his son's finances and property. Marco had only a credit card drawn on an account from which he could take just enough cash to live on. In fact, Pantani told friends several times that he had sold one of his two Ferraris to raise more cash.

Manuela Ronchi invited Marco to Milan again. She hoped that living a simple family life in a home with a new baby would bring balance to his life. No such luck. His father traveled to Milan to see him. Marco was elusive, indecisive, and distant. He left the Ronchi house and checked into the 289-room Jolly Hotel Touring near Milan's central train station and stayed there a week. "What hit me was that he hardly ever left his room and didn't come down to the restaurant," said hotel manager Maurizio Cossetti. "By all accounts, he was having a lot of problems."

THEN, ON FEBRUARY 9, Marco went to the station and boarded a train to the coastal town of Rimini. It was the last journey of his life. Perhaps he already knew that. He arrived by taxi at a modest residential hotel, Le Rose, which overlooked a deserted and melancholy beach. Pantani had no suitcases with him, nor his cell phone, just a bag containing two pairs of pants, some sneakers, and a few sweaters. "He simply asked for a room, any room," revealed hotel manager Sandro De Luigi, who gave Marco the key to a room on the fifth floor valued at 55 euros a night. The next day, February 10, Pantani phoned a childhood friend, Gloria, and told her candidly, "I'm not doing well."

In the last five days of his life, Pantani made four phone calls. They were all very brief, because the hotel computer registered less than 20 cents for each one. Just enough time to say a phrase or two. He extended his stay day by day. He twice made withdrawals of 20,000 euros (about $25,000) from his account, probably to buy drugs. He spent most days locked in his room, D5.

"He kept the room very hot," said Larissa Boyko, a Ukrainian housemaid who cleaned the fifth-floor rooms. "Sometimes he stared at me and asked if he scared me."

On Wednesday, February 11, he came down to breakfast and chatted briefly with two basketball players from the local Rimini club who were living at the hotel. Then, on Friday the 13th, Pantani again had breakfast and immediately returned to his room. Later in the day, he went to the nearby Rimini Key restaurant, whose owner, Oliver Langhi, made him a cheese-and-ham omelet. It was Marco's first square meal since arriving in Rimini . . . and also his last. "I personally took the plate to him," said Langhi. "I had trouble recognizing him. I said to him, 'This is on the house. Good luck, Marco, you're the best!' When he left, he tapped me on the shoulder and then almost closed the door in my face."

Back at the hotel, Marco bumped into a young man in the corridor outside his room. It was a 27-year-old student named Gianandrea who reported that Pantani said to him, in the local Romagnol dialect, *"A ne so se ui serà un elt dé"* ("I don't know if there will be another day"). The student shuddered as he remembered those tragic words, which are symptomatic of a person hounded by death. He was the last person to see Marco Pantani alive.

Gianandrea had come to pick up a friend who was staying in the room next to Marco's. He remembered that Marco "was wearing a rumpled shirt and was only half-shaven, his face very thin. He acted strangely, mumbling half phrases of no particular significance. At one point, he looked at us strangely and said, 'I've known you for a long time.' That's impossible. I'd never seen him before in my life. But I let it drop . . . he wasn't in a normal state.

"We spoke for about five minutes. He alternated between moments of lucidity and incoherence. About doping, he said to me, 'Once they've decided to eliminate you, they eliminate you.' Then he asked where we were going. 'What are you doing now? If there's a party, I'll join you. But after the evening's over . . . '"

The next morning, Saturday, February 14, Valentine's Day, Marco telephoned the receptionist, asking that no one come to clean his room. He then left the phone off the hook, not wanting to be disturbed. He replied from behind his locked door to the two basketball players who asked him how he was doing with silence.

At nine o'clock that night, the night receptionist went up to the room to take clean towels. He knocked on the door, but there was no reply. The door was apparently blocked by furniture so he decided to force his way in. The room was a mess, the bed still made. Pantani hadn't slept in it, having preferred to lie on the covers to watch TV. On the floor were a dozen jars of drugs: antidepressants, sedatives, even a box of women's contraceptive pills. On the table was the passport in which he had scribbled his final thoughts. There were traces of white powder. Marco's body lay at the foot of the bed. He was bare chested, wearing only jeans. He was thin again, just like a racer in training. His goatee was shaved clean. His lips were stained with blood. A bruise had made his face swell. Marco Pantani was dead.

HOW DID ONE OF THE GREATEST cyclists in history, a rider who was capable of exerting a magnetic attraction on millions of people, arrive at this point of degradation? Why was he staying alone in a 300-square-foot room, only 20 kilometers away from his splendid villa in Cesenatico, at the same time so close to everything yet so far away from the real world? He didn't kill himself, but what caused him to die?

Death in the Afternoon

Marco Pantani's life ended at about four o'clock in the afternoon on Saturday, February 14, 2004, some five hours before his body was discovered in his fifth-floor room at Le Rose hotel in Rimini. As soon as news of his death hit the airwaves, the outpouring of grief and recognition for the Italian cyclist was instant. Just as people around the world remember where they were when President Kennedy was assassinated in 1963, so cycling fans remember what they were doing at the moment they heard that Pantani was dead.

Crowds soon gathered opposite the hotel on the avenue Regina Elena in Rimini, staring up at the window of room D5. Saturday night traffic was at a standstill. Federal and municipal police officers blocked the hotel entrance, while reporters crowded outside. When Pantani's sister, Manola, arrived sometime after midnight, she had to fight her way through a phalanx of journalists, shouting, *"Andate via!"* ("Go away!").

When his body was removed from the hotel in the early hours of the next morning, a couple of hundred people still stood in the street, applauding, as the ambulance departed. Pantani remains an icon to the general public, especially in Italy, despite the frequent doping allegations against him and the subsequent hounding of him by the Italian judicial system.

The autopsy performed by Dr. Giuseppe Fortuni, a professor at the University of Bologna, revealed that Pantani had suffered a heart attack caused by severe swelling of the heart and brain. The exact cause of death wasn't reported until five months later, following an investigation by the state prosecutor, Paolo Gengarelli. Gengarelli's investigation implicated five people in Pantani's death. Three of them—Italians Fabio Carlino, Fabio Miradossa, and Ciro Veneruso—were accused of supplying cocaine directly to Pantani, while the cyclist's Russian friend, Elena Korovina, and a male friend were accused of complicity in the supply and trafficking of drugs. The fate of these five individuals was still unclear ten months after the February 2004 tragedy.

"In the final period of his life," wrote Dr. Fortuni, "Pantani had grave psychological problems derived from a massive consumption of cocaine. Very large quantities were found in his system—he died from an overdose. In such conditions, the question of suicide is absolutely unimaginable."

The doctor also ruled out the use of EPO as a factor in the cyclist's death. Dr. Fortuni reported, "Pantani had a bone structure that excluded all probability of EPO use, at least in the final months of his life."

Pantani's death instigated an outpouring of grief and tributes. His Mercatone Uno team director, Giuseppe Martinelli, said, "For those who loved him there is only one word: tragedy. He made a whole country cry with joy, even now. He was a phenomenon. I'll also send a request. Don't make mistakes when talking about him, because he was a giant."

Felice Gimondi, the 1965 Tour de France champion who in his role as the Bianchi marketing manager worked closely with Pantani, said, "He paid too high a price. For four years he was at the eye of the storm after having been *numero uno*. I'm in shock. I never expected anything like this."

One of Pantani's closest teammates, Roberto Conti, commented on the underground world of recreational drugs that brought about his friend's death. "I've heard enough talk that our [cycling] world is a den of drugs. But we [the riders] were the first to want coordinated blood and urine tests. I live here in Romagna, and I'm scared of the discotheques because that is where they dish out false values, not in the sport of cycling."

Another of Italy's major sports figures, retired skier Alberto Tomba, whose iconic status equals Pantani's, said, "I'm speechless. This is a real tragedy. I knew Pantani well. I believe he was alone at the very time he was in need of help."

Damiano Zoffoli, the mayor of Pantani's hometown, talked about another facet of Pantani's character. "I stayed close to him, even in his most difficult times," he said. "I will remember him as a very charitable young man. Few people knew that he worked for a group that helped handicapped people, and this town, which lives by tourism, owes him a lot. Many people have benefited from his exploits."

A boyhood friend, Cesare Cortesi, added, "What I really remember about Marco is when he was a small boy, he often got into fights with guys twice his size. They'd throw him to the ground. But he always got up. He was short in stature but battled like a lion."

It was Pantani's underdog ability to overcome seemingly superior opponents that had endeared him to the *tifosi*. During his winning performance, especially at the Giro d'Italia, crowds would mob his hotel every day, with children and their parents wanting to touch him as if he were the pope rather than a simple cyclist.

Humiliated by his very public condemnation in the media after Madonna di Campiglio, Pantani withdrew into a solitary world to which he returned again and again. It looked as though he had shaken off his demons in the spring of 2003 when he returned to racing after a ten-month absence.

A crash on a snow-lined alpine descent prevented Pantani from finishing in the top 10 at the 2003 Giro, the final race of his life.

He showed that he had worked extremely hard through the winter to find a level of fitness that he hadn't demonstrated since before his first brush with drug infamy at the Giro four years earlier.

Pantani started the 2003 Giro determined to prove that he was still worthy of the status of contender, and he was eager to go on to ride the centennial Tour de France. Many saw his former drive and determination return at the Giro, particularly when he attacked on the steep climb to the Zoncolan summit and showed he was one of the five strongest in the race. A scary crash on a snow-lined descent on the second-to-last alpine stage prevented Pantani from taking a top-10 finish in Milan, but 14th place overall was a worthy result for a rider making a comeback.

Two weeks later, after being snubbed by the Tour de France organizers, Pantani's depression returned, and he entered the downward spiral that ended in off-season Rimini on a dismal February afternoon. The staff at Le Rose, where Pantani lived as a recluse for the final five days of his life, said he seemed "out of it." They didn't know to what degree that was true. One of the most charismatic and most misunderstood characters in the history of cycling had become a victim of his own fame. That high hematocrit reading on June 5, 1999, may not have been a true conspiracy to bring him down, but it was the catalyst that led to his ultimate demise.

Marco and Lance

EVEN LANCE ARMSTRONG removed his hat. Faced with death, all rivalries fade into nothingness. Death softens all.

Lance had already been in Spain for a few days, and today he would be in Portugal to make his season debut at the Volta a Algarve. The Texan heard Saturday night of Marco Pantani's passing and immediately made a call to Italy to find out what happened. He wanted details. He asked, "How?" How could it have happened?

The rivalry between Armstrong and Pantani at the 2000 Tour was the most fierce and captivating in recent years. It was the meeting of the strongest personalities in the peloton.

Early yesterday morning, when Lance awoke, Marco was at the center of his thoughts. He called the *Gazzetta dello Sport* to express how disturbed he was about the death of a 34-year-old man. "I think about his family, his friends. Cycling is only part of life. I didn't think it could get so bad. Any new developments? Does anyone know anything more?"

Armstrong then synthesized his thoughts in the following official statement: "It's terrible and shocking news. My condolences go to his family, his friends, and all of his fans. Aside from our battles on and off the bike, I can say that I have always had deep respect for Marco. Cycling has lost a great champion and a great personality."

Marco was so similar to and different from Lance that their paths were destined to cross one another and transform their bikes into swords.

There had been a sort of mutual intrigue from the time they raced as amateurs. Marco had heard people talk about the talented Texan, and Lance had heard people talk about the kid from the coast who accomplished extraordinary feats in the mountains. In 1993, Armstrong won the world championship title in Oslo at the age of 21. In 1994, Pantani, at 24, brought Induráin to his knees at the Giro, finishing second in the *corsa rosa* on the heels of Evgueni Berzin.

The two kept track of each other, but their paths didn't cross. Up to that point, Lance had been a champion of one-day races. Then there was the cancer. Pantani, a man of great sensitivity, was one of the most concerned. But he wasn't the type to show his feelings—he was never able to.

When Lance found himself without a team, though, dropped by Cofidis, Marco asked his Mercatone Uno team to extend a hand to the Texan. He wanted Armstrong as a teammate.

Instead the Texan became the captain of the U.S. Postal team and within a period of two years became Mr. Tour. Armstrong was *Il Pirata*'s successor in the French race's hall of fame. He won the 1999 edition while Marco was still nursing the emotional wounds inflicted by his exclusion from the Giro d'Italia.

They raced together again in 2000 and sparks flew. Lance let Marco win the legendary stage on Mont Ventoux, which resulted in a controversy. Pantani was too proud to accept gifts. He set things right at Courchevel, he explained, which was his last great success. Those were explosive days for the dueling pair.

To provoke Marco, Lance referred to him as *Elefantino*, an obvious reference to the Romagnol's big ears. Marco simply referred to him as *l'Americano*.

The following year, at the start of the new season, Lance Armstrong wanted to arrange a meeting to clear things up with Pantani. He asked journalists at the *Gazzetta dello Sport* to set it up. They met at the Rincon de Pepe bar in the center of Murcia, Spain.

It was a meeting between two men who wanted to look each other in the eye and say exactly what they thought of one another. At a certain point, Lance looked at Marco and said, "Don't withdraw with your bad thoughts. Forget about everything that's happened to you. Think about winning. In a few years, not many, we'll be sitting on a beach somewhere laughing and drinking margaritas."

Marco didn't take that advice. Marco turned more and more inward until he couldn't take it anymore.

The Final Journey

CESENATICO, ITALY *February 18, 2004*

UP UNTIL THEN, SHE HAD KEPT HER COMPOSURE, but when Marco's final resting place, an elegant white ash coffin, was placed down in front of Niche 262, Mamma Tonina couldn't hold it in any longer. "I've been saying it for ten years. I knew my son would suffer the same fate as Coppi," she wailed as she embraced the coffin in tears, as one would a last, desperate illusion. "But now I want his words to make an impact. I want his dignity. I want it back," she continued before fainting. It took her a little while to recover. It will take a lifetime for her to find peace.

"His words" were those Marco nervously wrote on nine pages of his passport. They were thoughts listed one by one, perhaps on different occasions, last December in Cuba. And now they sound like a testament. They are a map of the hardships that caused the guy from Cesenatico to lose contact with reality . . . with life.

All you need to do is read between the lines of those notes in the disfigured passport. All you have to do is want to understand in order to perceive that Marco was headed down a dead-end road. He wrote, "They have

Roses covered the white ash coffin on its journey from the San Giacomo church to Cesenatico's cemetery.

humiliated me . . . I feel betrayed. . . ." He wrote of "dreams that are shattered by drugs," and he asked one last time for help. "I'm not a phony. I feel betrayed and all those who believed I was telling the truth must speak out."

Manuela Ronchi, Pantani's ex-manager and friend, read those sometimes less than lucid phrases at the end of the funeral service, a funeral being followed by some 20,000 people. Pantani's fans had expressed themselves once again. They were civil but obviously angry, as well as sad.

Marco's family asked that the San Giacomo parish church not be open to the public. Inside, there was seating for 300. Everyone else followed the ceremony conducted by Bishop Antonio Lanfranchi from outside.

The light-colored wood casket carrying the body of Marco Pantani lay in the center of the small church of familial simplicity. The jerseys that chronicled *Il Pirata's* career were on display: the white-and-blue jersey of the Fausto Coppi Cycling School of Cesenatico, the blue Italian team jersey from the 1995 world championships in Colombia, and the pink-and-yellow jerseys of his extraordinary 1998 season. Overhead and all around were roses, mostly yellow, his favorite color. Amid the wreaths there was even one with the colors of the Milan soccer team, and a touching one with the intimate signature "Your teacher."

The Pantani family entered the church shortly before Mass, around 2:25 P.M. Mamma Tonina took her place in the middle of the first row and spent the entire duration of the service with her head on Papà Ferdinando's shoulder, her left hand on Manola's shoulder.

Behind them sat Charly Gaul, the legendary climber and 1958 Tour de France champion from Luxembourg for whom Pantani had had a soft spot and who reciprocated the sentiment in full. Despite his frail physical condition, the 71-year-old Gaul remained standing for the entire service to pay tribute to Marco.

The world of cycling was well represented, both by past champions like Vittorio Adorni, Gianni Motta, Francesco Moser, Moreno Argentin, Davide Cassani, Silvio Martinello, Gianni Bugno, Evgueni Berzin, and Ivan Gotti and by many of today's big names, including Stefano Garzelli, Michele Bartoli, Alessandro Petacchi, Danilo Di Luca, Ivan Quaranta, and Filippo Pozzato. And there were many of Marco's most loyal *domestiques*: Siboni, Fontanelli, Borgheresi, Brignoli, Traversoni, Podenzana, Della Vedova, Caravaggio, and Artunghi, among others. Also there were team directors Alfredo Martini, Franco Ballerini, Davide Boifava, and Giuseppe Martinelli, along with Romano Cenni, the distraught president of Mercatone Uno; Giancarlo Ceruti, president of the Italian national cycling federation (who remained outside the church); Amedeo Colombo of the association of bicycle racers; and Jean-Marie Leblanc's assistant director of the Tour de France, Jean-François Pescheux. Carmine Castellano, director of the Giro d'Italia, was stuck in traffic because of an accident.

"Marco was a giant," said his former team director, Davide Boifava, here (right) in happier times.

In his eulogy, Bishop Lanfranchi said that he was "moved and uplifted by Pantani's great accomplishments" but also "saddened by his misfortunes," and went on to emphasize that "Marco's death is a call for serious soul-searching with regard to what is going on in the world of sports. A person is greater than any victory, and any defeat. A person is worth more than the sport of cycling and should not be sacrificed to any type of exploitation." Then he added that "Marco's death also serves as a call for friendship: for the gift of friendship and of hope. That no one be alone. That no one feel or be left alone. We must believe in life with the same passion that Marco demonstrated in accomplishing his victories."

The bishop talked about values, and that Pantani had unfortunately lost his way over the past four years. Now there was a morbid process of trying to understand how, why, or by whose fault Marco would tarnish his stardom in turning to cocaine for comfort. How and why Marco became numb to the affection of family and friends, even of those he cherished most, until it killed him while he was alone, on Valentine's Day, in an obscure hotel room facing the winter sea.

In the church, many were crying. Sabrina, his former Tuscan sweetheart, who became Marco's fiancée before the accident at the 1995 Milan-Turin, was there with a child in her arms. She remembered Marco with a silence punctuated by long streams of tender tears. At the end of the Mass, the mayor of Cesenatico, Damiano Zoffoli, and Don Agostino, for many years connected to the local parish, spoke about "their" Pantani.

Then Marco took center stage again, with one last exploit, an unexpected and theatrical entrance. In his long journey toward nothingness, the kid from the coast had found himself confronted with the person he had become and wanted to record it for posterity. This tortured journey in search of truth was translated into a series of thoughts scribbled into his passport during his second trip to Cuba.

> "A person is greater than any victory, and any defeat. A person is worth more than the sport of cycling and should not be sacrificed to any type of exploitation."

When Michel, his friend from Predappio with whom he had lived the summer before, and another friend, a restaurateur, went to the land of Fidel Castro to fetch Marco, they found themselves faced with an unexpected problem. Because of the transformation of his passport into a diary, Marco would have risked not being able to go home had the border inspector not been a Pantani fan (Marco had ripped out some of the pages of his passport and thrown them in a trash bin, where Michel went to recover them). Manuela Ronchi, her voice trembling with emotion, attempted to read those phrases exactly as Marco would have.

*Three weeks after Pantani's death, the toughest mountain stage of Spain's Tour of Murcia—
one of Marco's favorite races—was won by fellow Italian Danilo Di Luca (pictured with one of
Pantani's former team managers, Giuseppe Martinelli). Pantani was honored, too.*

As a synopsis, they are the key to understanding his distant suffering. Marco continued to feel that his pride had been deeply wounded on that sad morning in Madonna di Campiglio. He never accepted that loss of dignity. But every time he hung his head, Marco seemed to launch a new attack and get back in the saddle. He asked for "rules that apply to everyone equally." He complained of "public and private lives being violated" and, deep down, he tried to justify turning to drugs for help in facing his unease.

It was with Marco's phrases fresh in their minds that the very long funeral procession arrived at the Cesenatico cemetery. The bier was carried on the shoulders of Marco's *domestiques* and friends, until it arrived at Niche 262, just above Grandpa Sotero, a figure larger than life in Marco's world. The cemetery niche of the kid from Cesenatico was sealed at 5:30 P.M. If he had been able to see Grandpa Sotero's photograph below, with the big hat and familiar sneer, he would have given his fans the gift of one last charismatic and mischievous smile.

Christina's Confessions

Marco Pantani's longtime Danish girlfriend Christina Jonsson gave only one interview after his death. She spoke to Swiss journalist Michel Beuret of the weekly magazine, L'Hebdo.

<u>LAUSANNE</u> *April 2004*

CHRISTINA JONSSON WAS MARCO PANTANI'S girlfriend for seven years. Before his tragic death in February 2004, Marco wrote how much he missed her. He and Christina had split reluctantly the previous summer. But she remained the one love of his life, the witness to his immense glory, and the closest observer of his downward path since he was expelled from the Giro d'Italia in June 1999.

We met with Christina in Lausanne, where she now lives and works as a painter. Since the champion's death, the paparazzi had searched everywhere for her, but in vain. At first the young Danish woman wanted to remain quiet about the intimacy she had shared with The Pirate, but the media wouldn't leave her alone. In the end, she decided to talk. One interview, just once. Through a mutual friend, she contacted the author at *L'Hebdo.* The result was this extraordinary interview.

Christina's narrative is revealing. Yes, Marco did dope, she said, but just like all the others; and, yes, he consumed "industrial quantities" of cocaine after 1999. And through her love for him, she plunged into his pain and paranoia. But this testimony did not come easily from her. Christina wasn't prepared.

145

The interview resulted from five visits, with long conversations making up each session. Several times the interview was interrupted because the pain was too strong. She would choke up. She spoke of the three years of good times, the crash, the forced silences, and the siege by 200 journalists around their home.

Her words also provide clues to understanding and sometimes determining the way in which an infernal system leads champions to take more and more risks in search of performances that are ever more lucrative. A system that demands doping and yet fights it. A system that on the one hand is money and silence and on the other provides new gladiators as fodder for the fans.

Soccer star Diego Maradona was another victim of this system. He also happened to be a hero of Pantani's, with whom he shared a similar destiny: an impoverished childhood, a remarkable success, a downward spiral, and at the end, solitude and cocaine. The two men met once in Cuba just before Pantani's death. On his return to Italy, Marco wrote the now-famous testament in his passport: "But what's left? There is so much sadness and anger as a result of the injustices. . . . But I hope my story will serve as an example for other sports; rules, yes, but they should be the same for everyone."

Christina told us about so much sadness and anger, and love, too.

The paparazzi looked for you everywhere in Italy and here you are in Switzerland.
Yes, I live in Lausanne.

Just before he died, Marco Pantani left a message for you.
Yes, I know. But this message didn't reach me. Our love relationship ended definitively in the summer of 2003. After that, I only got news of him by telephone.

He was the love of your life?

Yes, He was my first serious love, and we matured together; it was a merging love. In addition, I gave myself the responsibility of saving him. I always thought that I would return to live with him one day, when he succeeded in stopping the drugs. Even on the day he died, before I heard the news, I felt a strong urge to see him again.

How did you find out about his death?

I had a call from a friend in Italy. It had been about two months since Marco and I had spoken. I haven't stopped crying. Confronting death, there's nothing you can say. At that moment, I was in Switzerland where I was preparing my thesis for the fine arts academy in Ravenna.

Why have you remained quiet until now?

It's true. I've done everything to avoid the media. You can't imagine what they are capable of in Italy. Fame makes people go crazy there. A Danish proverb says it all: "When the sun shines on you, it also shines on the one at your side." Marco was that sunshine, and he helped a lot of people get tan. It was for that reason that they pursued me.

Did you go to his funeral?

No, I would have liked to have seen Marco one last time before they buried him. But I understood I couldn't go when I learned it was going to be a public burial. In Italy, certain newspapers wrote that I was responsible for Marco's death because I left him, and I learned that angry fans and the paparazzi were waiting for me there. I didn't have the courage to face them. Also, there was a private ceremony reserved for the extended family. But I didn't receive an invitation. . . . Those were extremely painful times.

They still pursued you.

Yes, after his death was announced, journalists were calling from all over. To my friends in Italy, and even back to Denmark. My roommate in Ravenna suffered enormously. She had to leave the house. Other people in my circle were offered as much as 3,000 euros just to get my phone number. Nobody gave it, but they contacted everyone I know. But that didn't stop newspapers' attributing quotes to me, even though I hadn't spoken to them. *Oggi* magazine even published a photo of the place where Marco died with a woman supposed to be me whose face was hidden. An inspector from Rimini, where Marco died, called me on a friend's telephone in Switzerland to ask if I had met Marco one Valentine's Day, a February 14. On checking, it was definitely the police. So I told him to write to me and gave him my address in Lausanne. The next day, the paparazzi arrived. They came into the art school where I was painting and started filming without any authorization. These intrusions couldn't continue. So I decided to speak.

So, let's start at the beginning. How did you meet Marco in the first place?

In fairly unusual circumstances. It was in 1996 at a Cesenatico discotheque. I worked as a professional dancer. In Italy, that's very fashionable. They call them the "cubists" because the girls dance on a cubical podium. One evening, Marco came. He had broken a leg and was still using crutches to walk. He was with his friends.

Had you heard of him at that point?

No, I'd only been in Italy eight months. I was 19 and just arrived from Denmark. After graduating from high school, I left my family to live a different life in another country. That's when I met him. He was 26. Little by little, we got to know each other. Being a full-time cyclist since his adolescence, he hadn't had much experience of late-night partying. The accident had allowed him to live differently. The Marco that I met then was a person still finding his feet. On one hand, with his injury, he was worried about his future and fighting internally. On the other, he overcame his fears to make the most of his life.

Why did you leave Denmark?
I wanted to see other cultures, and I had a friend in Italy who made her living as a dancer. It's a real career there. At my age, it was a dream, to get paid for having fun. At first, I went to Riccione, the party capital of the Adriatic coast. Then I made a tour around the whole country working as a dancer before ending up in Cesenatico, where I met Marco.

An elite sportsman always on the road, a nightclub dancer, how did you reconcile these two different lives?
After three or four months of dating, we decided that I would come to live in his town, and leave my Riccione apartment. So we set up house together. That lasted a few months. At that moment—it was a delicate situation—his mother felt put out that her son had left the family home for a person she didn't know. And then I was only 19. I was a girl from northern Europe, a dancer, something of a rebel. Like many parents, they worried about their son's future. That led Marco to move back in with his parents, and I went with him. That lasted six months, and then I decided that it was best if I lived alone.

You didn't plan to live together?
Yeah, we thought about it, but we were afraid to live as a couple, as adults. Marco had already bought some land to build a house. One part reserved for his parents, the other for him. Eventually, I joined him there.

149

Did you carry on dancing?

No, I wanted to be with Marco as much as possible, and so be around in the daytime. I'd had enough of the nightclub scene.

So what did you do then?

I wanted to go back to work and my studies. At first, in 1997, I served in an ice cream shop. Then Marco suggested I work at the family *piadina* [flatbread stand]. At first, I didn't think this was a good idea. But I went anyway. I worked for them three years. And it was in 1998 that I started school as an art student.

Did you feel the family really accepted you?

It wasn't always easy.

You like the arts. Were you at all interested in sports?

No, I was never interested, not even bike racing. I've never believed in results, nor competition, nor in making a lot of money. I'm not a competitive person. But as that was Marco's motivation and that's how he lived, I supported him as much as I could.

Did you go to follow him at the grand tours in France and Italy?

Not very often. He didn't need to have someone always at his side. And then, I had my work at the *piadina*, so I could only travel for a day or two at a time. But, as we know, the cycling world has a hard time accepting girlfriends at races. And Marco needed his space to concentrate. Many times that stopped him from calling me.

What was daily life like with him?

He was often away. And when he returned, it was to get some rest. He needed to recuperate for the next race. He often arrived home so tired that he could only collapse on the bed. He was a very determined and courageous person.

Did you want to see him more than you did?

Naturally. I hoped that one day we could both be together more often and that things would be more calm. So we could have a better life. I hoped that after these years dedicated to his career, he would be able to do something different. But since we were first together, I said to myself, "Okay, for the moment, it's his wish to win races and work hard. I have to understand that."

That work also enabled him to earn a lot of money.

For sure. What he did made him very rich, and he knew what he was worth This factor was even more important because he came from a fairly poor family. He knew about the hard times his parents went through when he was little. So that was a motivation to get to the top.

What was Marco like when he returned home after winning a big race? Was he euphoric?

No, once a race was over, he was already preparing for the next. One win was never enough. It was as if there was a motor inside him that kept him going. He was a perfectionist.

Did he sometimes have some cycling buddies over at the house?

In fact, he had a fairly limited social life. On one side there was the cycling world, on the other was relaxation. At least, that was how I saw things. For sure he had several friends in the peloton, like Siboni, Fontanelli, and Conti. But few of them lived near us. When he was at the house, he spent a lot of time alone.

What did he like to do besides cycling?

He adored Ferraris, Porsches. He loved the speed for sure, the adrenaline rush. Other than that, he liked simple things. He was very traditional. He liked fixing things around the house, but didn't have much time. He also adored hunting and fly fishing. He knew the names of every fish. We would go together sometimes. There again, he was passionate about it. Even tying the smallest knot, he took the time to be very precise. He also enjoyed mechanical things, technology. Until 1999, he would take apart his bike and reassemble it every day. He would constantly make changes to it, always looking for more efficient parts. He would adjust his saddle by 3 or 4 millimeters, and that's nothing to what he would do to his shoes! Everything was in flux, day and night. He always wanted to know that he could make improvements. As for me, I adored this enthusiasm for the smallest detail.

You're describing an almost obsessed personality.

It was a means for him to excel. I don't want to treat psychology lightly; I'm not a doctor. But in hindsight, I think that this discipline enabled him to fight against a form of depression. His profession allowed him to channel that. That's my theory, maybe it's a little rough, but that's what I believe. His fabulous success came from his extraordinary need to fight an inferiority complex.

A revenge for his childhood?

Let's say he had a need to be liked and accepted every time he won.

Was Marco a generous person?

Yes, very generous, but not in the sense of a big spender. Besides the house he had built for his family and his cars, he didn't squander his money. He was generous in the true sense of the word. He gave of himself.

Loyal?

Yes, in every sense of the word, with me, with his friends, with his family. It was important for Marco to work with people he had confidence in, and it was difficult to separate him from them. When he felt confidence in someone, he could forgive them for anything. He gave loyalty the highest value, simply because it was difficult for him to build it. Lots of people abused his gentleness.

You say he had traditional values, but in cycling he played the part of the aggressor, the "pirate."

Yes, that's true. The world of cycling is conservative, and Marco was a rebel in that world. He didn't want to be a cyclist just like the others. He *wasn't* a cyclist just like the others. He had a certain view of this milieu, and he wanted to change it. That's why he was the first to play with his image.

Because his ears stuck out, journalists had once called him Elefantino.

He had them operated on in 2003, in the middle of his depression, but I adored his ears! When I met him, he already had his earring and bandanna. He was already The Pirate. Then he added a tattoo under his eyes, an eyeliner, to emphasize the look. That amused him. He loved to provoke.

He liked to sing, too, no?

Yes. He loved Italian music. Pop music. He also liked to sing in karaoke bars. In 1996, after he had the operation on his leg, he even recorded a song that was played every day at the Giro. He decided to do that because he was so bummed that he couldn't participate. The fans loved it.

He was a sort of artist.

I would say yes. He had little interest in the arts in general and even less for my abstract canvases! But in his own manner, yeah, he had something of the artist in him. He was always on the lookout for something new, never satisfied. He always went above and beyond, to transcend himself. In that, we were similar. I always wanted to know myself better, and I discovered that Marco, in private, pursued the same search of identity.

What did he like in you?

I think at first that it was the joyful part of my personality. Politically incorrect, too. And then I'm Danish, from a different culture, and I push aside convention. He did the same to me. When I arrived in his family, it seemed normal to him that I would do the dishes, the laundry, make meals, etcetera. For him, that was women's work.

Conservative at home, extrovert outside?

I don't know if you would say that. But if you want to.

Was he interested in your work at the art school?

Yes, but more likely in a critical way. He didn't like the school. . . . He had a hard time understanding contemporary art and my work at the academy. Like he was jealous. He was afraid I would meet someone there. But little by little he saw that the studies made me happy. What I like in art is the game, the expression, the research. I also had that outlook when I danced. In fact, the result itself has little importance.

That's the opposite of a champion's attitude, that only the result counts.

Yes, that's true.

We're in 1999. Marco Pantani has become a great champion, winner of the 1998 Tour de France and Giro d'Italia. And then suddenly, a blood test is above the legal limit. Marco is thrown out of the Giro. What did he do?

He returned home and spent days in despair and crying. He was completely paralyzed. We couldn't even go out. At least 150 to 200 journalists surrounded the house.

Did he talk to you at that time?

Hardly at all. Marco felt betrayed and abandoned. He felt that his exclusion was premeditated, that it was a conspiracy against him. And looking at the facts, witnesses can conclude that he had good reason. After Marco's death, his teammate Marco Velo confided to a newspaper that on June 4, 1999, the day before [the blood test and] Marco's exclusion, rumors were already circulating that he would not be continuing. At that moment, Marco Pantani was about to win the Giro. He was in the pink jersey, and we were only two days from the finish. In Italy, huge bets were riding on the main players. . . .

What happened next?

Around the house, journalists had set up tents. It seemed interminable. They'd got out their long-range listening devices and set up their telephoto lenses in the ground to spy on the house. We could see them. Marco stayed secluded for four days in the dark, silent. I couldn't succeed in communicating with him. I despaired of him. I started working at the family stand again. I can't even begin to tell you how difficult that time was. Then Marco started going out again at night. After about ten days, he came to see me and said, "Listen. I've started taking cocaine."

Just like that? From one day to the next?

Yes.

But where did the cocaine come from?

I don't know. But it's not hard to find, you know. . . .

Why did he start to take drugs?

I believe that it was the only way for him to withstand the pressure, to survive the incredible pressure that was put on him. You can only imagine what it was like. One day before the exclusion, Marco was in brilliant physical shape, full of unimaginable energy; and, in the space of a few hours, he found himself stuck in his house with his whole world collapsed around him. He could display incredible physical violence and that soured our relationship.

How did you react?

I cried. I couldn't believe what had happened. I was in despair because I'm afraid of drugs. I know the effects of cocaine due to the prevention campaigns I'd witnessed from a young age in Denmark. In Italy, they know practically nothing. To consume cocaine is even somewhat fashionable, a sign of prosperity. And when Marco announced to me that he was taking cocaine . . . it was also to let me know that he wanted me to take it with him. If I loved him, I must do it. . . . I felt that he wanted me to partake. For him. He saw it as a demonstration of my love. He was alone, and he also believed that I had betrayed him, that I was unfaithful to him. That whole period was a nightmare.

Did you accept his "demand"?

Yes. For years I met plenty of people in nightclubs who took drugs without me touching them myself. And there I was drugged in that house. I was very fragile myself. Cocaine gave the illusion of having a great facility to communicate. It was, of course, pure fantasy. I thought that it would help me renew my connection with Marco. I wanted to rediscover him and bring him back to reality. I really wanted to live at his side once more. And I just plunged with him. I had reacted to a sort of blackmail, a way of functioning that I knew well from my father's place—I grew up with an alcoholic mother.

Did your sacrifice allow you to help him?
No, not at all. It was a terrible error to believe that. Until then, I had hoped that I would spend more time alone with him. Even at the house, with his parents, we were rarely alone. And then, after his exclusion from the Giro, we found ourselves together, just the two of us. I had my Marco, but we weren't doing well. I held out my hand; I wanted to show him my life. [*Christina could barely speak at this point.*] I wanted to get him away, make a trip together, change his ideas. But we were at the house, drugged, ringed by journalists. And Marco continued to believe I was unfaithful.

He was very jealous?
Incredibly jealous, since always. But then it was worse than ever. He'd become paranoid also. But I think life as a pro cyclist made him paranoid.

How so?
For a long time, he had lived in fear of the anti-doping controls in the stage hotels where he slept. Of these men who suddenly arrive, even at night. It's brutal. I witnessed one of these raids. They treat racers like criminals. All that made him paranoid. Suddenly, Marco had confidence in nobody, talking to very few people. He succeeded in handling his paranoia; he could live with it. But the cocaine, I'm certain, amplified the paranoid tendencies. And then

all those journalists around us at that moment. . . . He went as far as to imagine that they had installed electronic bugs in all the rooms and were spying on us. He believed he saw them climbing on the balcony. He locked all the doors.

In 1999, if he hadn't taken cocaine, what would he have done?

I don't know . . . perhaps he would have wanted to chuck it all in, to denounce the system. But I sensed he couldn't do that. That he didn't have the strength; he wasn't prepared for that. And then, as is known, he could imagine the impact of such revelations. His voice was a powerful one. His response was cocaine. That allowed him to run away from the world and the pressure, to live for four years beyond that world.

But you, did you stop using drugs?

I stopped after three months. Things had become unbearable. In the evening after work, we took cocaine together. Marco consumed industrial quantities. I was afraid. His body supported it. He had an exceptional physique. And then, very quickly, his parents realized that something was up. They weren't able to communicate with Marco and ended up working through me. And with me, their relationship was very ambiguous. On one hand, they needed me; on the other, I was an accomplice in their eyes. Where did the drug supply come from? Clearly, for the family, it was the fault of "la Christina, this dancer, this disco girl."

Did nobody come to see him at the house after 1999?

Yes, people dropped by, to encourage him, to ask him to start [racing] again. But his spirit was broken. He was furious with everyone. He said, "When I do well, you, the others, all do well. But if I fall, nobody knows what to do." And he had reason. Because everyone believed in Marco. We were all worried when he wasn't doing well and felt lost.

He was the inspiration for the whole region.
Everybody! The whole of Italy, his region, his team, his family. Everyone said to him, *"Ma dai Marco!* Get back in the saddle! We want to see the champion again." And he then felt responsible for all these people's anxieties.

He was accused of doping. What do you think, being the one who lived with him?
I think that he doped. Do you know any competitive athlete who doesn't dope? And "to dope"? What does that mean? Take products that are on the prohibited list? And why? To dope, that means searching to improve your performance to give a better show, to feed dreams. They pay these athletes because they allow people to dream, that's all. If there's no longer a show, there's no more emotion and nothing to relate to. All the rest is hypocrisy. Do you think it's possible to keep on improving a human being's physical performance year after year? And yet that's what everyone wants. In every sport. Like many others, I believe that Marco doped, yes. But in the end, that's nobody's business. People like to talk about doping and drugs and put the blame on someone else, to let steam off on someone to eliminate their own bad habits, their own misery, and for a moment to feel better. As long as he wins, he's our hero. If he falls, he becomes the black sheep, and we want black sheep. They throw stones at them because they say they're doped and everyone drags them through the shit without thinking—as if for pleasure.

And all this forced him to start doping?
I've no idea. Living with him, I always had the impression that Marco took drugs on his own, and that he determined the risks himself. It was his choice,

and I even have the impression that he paid for the products out of his own pocket. He didn't confide about this subject to many people, even to me. I sensed that he didn't even have confidence in the doctors on his own team. One day, he just let out that he had to take "junk" to be competitive. He was angry against the system and concerned about his health, I believe. He had these products forever in a sealed container in the fridge, but I was never interested enough to ask him what it was. That was Marco's life. He didn't want to talk about it, and I respected that. Sometimes, he injected himself, and I helped him by holding his arm. That's all.

But he took risks!

But he always did! He earned his living by taking risks. That was his job. You only had to see the speed at which he descended mountain roads. Marco had to accept to race in a system that didn't allow him not to dope. And, at the same time, it's a system that promotes anti-doping campaigns that put immense pressure on the riders. These same campaigns make the riders' health the supreme value.

You don't find this hypocritical?

But of course! An incredible hypocrisy! These pressures and implicit contradictions, these unspoken facts weighed on Marco to such a degree that in the end he couldn't withstand them. He took risks for others and then suffered from them. I understand that now. One or two months, I think it was, before the Giro blood test, I remember him saying to me, "I've had enough of all this. I can't do it any longer!" He wanted to disclose everything, pop the bubble. And then reality set in. I said to him, "If you stopped, what would you do?" He replied sarcastically, "Okay, I'll be a doctor. I'm better prepared than the average doctor." I wouldn't have dared to ask him to stop. . . . Cycling was his whole life.

Marco said that he had "served as a scapegoat. "

Exactly. And what was the hardest for him is the impression that those who also played the game stabbed him in the back. The anti-doping campaign had to make an example of him. Other, less well-known riders had already gone down, but no one could care less. It needed a star to make the headlines. Even the judges wanted to show everyone that they were courageous and had worked hard. And then Marco often told me that in Italy they focus on doping affairs in cycling to turn the attention away from soccer. Because in football there's much more at stake.

After 1999, did he ever give you hope?

Yes, many times. Marco did say, "I'm starting over." He thought that the bike could give him back the strength to overcome his depression and help him give up cocaine. So he got back in the saddle. He did several races and then relapsed. On returning home, the dealers contacted him, and it started again. They even came and knocked on his door. My life with Marco was a perpetual cycle of hope and despair, coming together and breaking apart. I really saw that I couldn't continue like that. Work, studies, withstand the crises. . . . It was too much. So in the summer of 2003, I left for good. To protect my health, both physically and mentally. To finish my thesis, too. I thought about myself.

So what have you done?

For some time I've left the family home. I lived in an apartment in Ravenna. The year 2003 was very important for me. I had to finish my work in fine arts, and I had missed a year because of the cocaine. To refocus, I had to be able to breathe. I had to leave. I came to Switzerland to see an art exhibition in Basel. It was there that I met David D'Ambrosio, director of the Tétard School in Lausanne. An amazing person.

When did you speak to Marco for the last time?

It was on my birthday in December. He called me to send his greetings. I have a wonderful memory of our conversation. He told me that he knew that I had met someone new, that he didn't want to intrude, that he hoped that everything was going well and that I was happy. . . . [*Christina broke into tears once more, exhausted.*]

How are you doing now?

Today my life is a bit like a dream for me, because for the first time I know what I want to do. And I'm starting to do it. During the time that I lived with Marco, I was still searching, and that makes you anxious. I wasn't too inspired by an Italian-style life: start a family and become a *mamma*. I just wanted to find a life that suited me.

You've found your path from now on?

During my studies, I had the chance to do some joint exhibits in Italy. Last October, I put on my first solo show at a gallery in Ravenna. In fact it was a three-day performance, fairly confrontational, provocative, and I had a lot of fun. It was like displaying the "cubist," the dancer, in a conservative gallery converted into a discotheque. Really, I'd like to put on an exhibition in Switzerland. Right now, I'm painting the adorable cows that I see in your fields. They're so "darling." It's "just like that" as you say here?

© 2004 Michel Beuret, *L'Hebdo*

Marco Pantani's Cycling Career

Born at Cesena, Italy, January 13, 1970

Died at Rimini, Italy, February 14, 2004

Lived at Cesenatico, Italy

Height: 5-foot-7

Racing weight: 125 pounds

Marco Pantani, known as *Il Pirata* (The Pirate), was the fastest climber of his generation, known for his incredible accelerations that left his opponents in the dust. In 1998 he became the first Italian since Felice Gimondi in 1965 to win the Tour de France, and became one of only seven men to win the Giro d'Italia and Tour in the same season.

PROFESSIONAL CYCLING CAREER DETAILS

1992   *Team: Carrera-Tassoni*

Pantani was 22 when he turned pro on August 5, 1992, after a successful amateur career that included an impressive victory in the amateur version of the Giro d'Italia.

Results:

8/29	Giro del Veneto, 20th
9/14	Memorial Nencini (Passo dell Futa), 3rd

1993 Team: Carrera-Tassoni

As a junior member of the Carrera team, Pantani started his first Giro d'Italia as a *domestique* for team leader Claudio Chiappucci. While Pantani pulled out of the race with tendinitis three days before the finish, Chiappucci placed third overall, 5:27 behind winner Miguel Induráin.

Results:

2/27	Giro della Provincia de Reggio di Calabria, 9th
4/5–9	Tour of the Basque Country, 19th
4/14	Flèche Wallonne, 30th
4/18	Liège-Bastogne-Liège, 67th
4/25	Giro di Friuli, 12th
5/1	GP Larciano, 6th
5/12–14	Giro del Trentino, 5th

1994 Team: Carrera-Tassoni

On his second appearance at the Giro d'Italia, Pantani blew the race apart in the Dolomites with back-to-back stage wins. He finished second overall behind the Russian Evgueni Berzin, with multi-Tour and multi-Giro champion Miguel Induráin in third. Pantani followed this with third place in his debut Tour de France. It was a sensational year for a second-year pro.

Results:

4/17	Liège-Bastogne-Liège, 67th
4/30	GP Prato, 6th
5/1	GP Larciano, 4th
5/11–13	Giro del Trentino, 4th
5/15	Tour of Tuscany, 4th
5/22–6/12	**Giro d'Italia, 2nd**
6/4	**Giro d'Italia, stage 14, 1st**
6/5	**Giro d'Italia, stage 15, 1st**
6/22	Italian Championship, 13th
7/2–24	**Tour de France, 3rd**
7/26	GP Callac, 4th
8/1	GP Château-Chinon, 3rd
8/21	Championship of Zürich, 71st
8/23	GP Luisiana, 12th

8/31   GP Innsbruck, 2nd

9/9   GP La Louvière, 4th

1995   *Team: Carrera-Tassoni*

A training crash on May 1 kept Pantani from riding the 1995 Giro, but he recovered in time for the Tour de France, claiming his first two mountain stage wins (including the prestigious Alpe d'Huez victory), and took 13th place overall.

In October he was one of the chief animators of the mountainous world road championship in Duitama, Colombia, taking the bronze medal behind Spaniards Abraham Olano and Miguel Induráin.

A week after returning from the 1995 world's in high-elevation Colombia, Pantani competed at the Milan-Turin race, a minor classic in Italy. On the fast descent into Turin, he was involved in a frightening head-on crash with an SUV, sustaining multiple fractures to his left leg that threatened his career.

In the Turin hospital, Pantani had the regulation blood tests, and several years later it was revealed that his blood hematocrit percentage following the accident was close to 60. Between the accident and the revelation four years later, the UCI had begun regular blood testing at races, and any rider caught with an above-50-percent reading was given a compulsory two-week suspension on the suspicion that the athlete was using the banned blood-boosting drug EPO. But even though that program didn't start until well after Pantani's accident, it didn't stop the Turin prosecutor from indicting Pantani on a so-called fraud in sport charge, a case that was eventually dismissed.

Results:

3/18   Milan–San Remo, 98th

4/12   Flèche Wallonne, 25th

4/16   Liège-Bastogne-Liège, 18th

4/25   Tour of the Apennines, 5th

5/1   (Training crash at San Arcangelo)

6/13–22 Tour of Switzerland, 17th

6/21   Tour of Switzerland, stage 9, 1st

6/25	Italian Championship, 16th
7/1–23	Tour de France, 13th
7/12	**Tour de France, stage 10, 1st**
7/15	**Tour de France, stage 14, 1st**
7/28	GP Geraardsbergen, 3rd
7/31	GP Castillon-la-Bataille, 3rd
8/6	GP St. Martin-de-Landelles, 3rd
8/9	GP Camaiore, 7th
8/12	Clasica San Sebastian, 38th
8/13	Subida a Urkiola, 6th
10/8	**World Road Championship, 3rd**
10/18	(Race crash at Milan-Turin)

1996 *Team: Carrera-Longoni*

Pantani fought back valiantly from his broken leg, suffering through months of rehab, much of it in a swimming pool, and made a tentative comeback to racing in August 1996.

Results:

8/3	(Return to racing at GP Cepagatti)

1997 *Team: Mercatone Uno*

On his return to the grand tours, Pantani crashed out of the 1997 Giro in a pileup caused by a black cat crossing the road on the descent from Chiunzi on the Amalfi coast. He returned to racing a month later at the Tour de France, and promptly took two more mountain stages (including Alpe d'Huez again) and finished third overall.

Results:

3/22	Milan–San Remo, 31st
3/24–27	Setmana Catalana, 10th
3/29–30	Critérium International, 4th
4/7–11	Tour of the Basque Country, 3rd
4/16	Flèche Wallonne, 5th
4/20	Liège-Bastogne-Liège, 8th
6/29	Italian Championship, 10th
7/5–27	**Tour de France, 3rd**

7/19	**Tour de France, stage 13, 1st**
7/21	**Tour de France, stage 15, 1st**
7/31	Across Lausanne, 2nd
8/1	Tony Rominger Classic, 1st
8/2	GP Pijnacker, 1st

1998 *Team: Mercatone Uno–Bianchi*

Injury-free at last, Pantani won 15 races in 1998. He won the Giro (and two stages) and the Tour (two more stages), coming back from a poor first week to take the yellow jersey from Jan Ullrich on a dramatic stage over the Galibier to Les Deux-Alpes. Pantani stood 4th in the UCI world rankings at the end of the year. The Pirate was praised for emerging as a beacon of hope from a Tour that endured the Festina team doping scandal.

Results:

3/4–8	Tour of Murcia, 3rd
3/7	Tour of Murcia, stage 4, 1st
4/27–30	Giro del Trentino, 4th
5/16–6/7	**Giro d'Italia, 1st**
5/30	**Giro d'Italia, stage 14, 1st**
6/4	**Giro d'Italia, stage 19, 1st**
6/8	GP Bologna, 1st
7/11–8/2	**Tour de France, 1st**
7/22	**Tour de France, stage 11, 1st**
7/27	**Tour de France, stage 15, 1st**
8/4	Across Lausanne, 1st
8/9	GP Charlottenlund, 1st
8/11	GP Surguisterveen, 1st
8/24	GP Châteaulin, 1st
9/20	Luxembourg-Steinsel, 1st
9/27	Crans-Montana, 1st
10/25	GP Valencia, 1st

1999 *Team: Mercatone Uno–Bianchi*

In June, Pantani appeared headed for another overall win at the Giro, having won four mountain stages and holding a lead of 5:38 over the runner-up.

Then, only two days from the finish, a blood test at Madonna di Campiglio showed that he had an above-the-50-percent-limit hematocrit reading. The automatic 14-day suspension put him out of the race. Shattered by the experience, disgraced in the media, even though he had never tested positive at any drugs control (he still hadn't at the time of his death), Pantani went into a deep depression and did not race again in 1999.

Results:

3/3–7	Tour of Murcia, 1st
3/6	Tour of Murcia, stage 4, 1st
3/20	Milan–San Remo, 62nd
3/23	Setmana Catalana, stage 2, 1st
4/9	Tour of the Basque Country, 8th
5/22	**Giro d'Italia, stage 8, 1st**
5/30	**Giro d'Italia, stage 15, 1st**
6/6	**Giro d'Italia, stage 19, 1st**
6/7	**Giro d'Italia, stage 20, 1st**

2000 *Team: Mercatone Uno*

The Pirate made his big comeback at the 2000 Giro, which he rode for training. Then, at the Tour, he won two mountain stages, ahead of Lance Armstrong, on Mont Ventoux and at Courchevel. He followed this with a long, brave (some said foolish) attack on the next stage to Morzine. Pantani's aggression split apart the race, and even though he himself eventually blew up, his effort caused Armstrong's Postal team to make an all-day chase through the mountains; Armstrong bonked on the day's last climb, putting his yellow jersey in jeopardy. Pantani pulled out of the Tour the next morning.

Results:

5/13–6/4	Giro d'Italia, 28th
7/13	**Tour de France, stage 12, 1st**
7/16	**Tour de France, stage 15, 1st**
7/25	GP Stiphout, 1st
7/26	Aacht de Chaam, 1st
9/16	Giro del Lazio, 34th
9/27	Olympic Road Race, 69th

In 1998, Marco Pantani became only the third cyclist in history to win the Tour de France and Giro d'Italia in the same year.

2001   *Team: Mercatone Uno*

Pantani was still not over his depression, and he began the 2001 Giro with a lack of racing miles, but made an impression on the opening road stage when he attacked in a rainstorm and helped create a major breakaway. He soon faded, however, and was about to pull out of the race when the police raids of riders' hotels took place. Pantani was among the 50 or so people who were listed on the suspicion of possessing banned substances. He was then one of the few singled out by the prosecutor, as there were traces of insulin on a syringe found in his hotel room.

Results:

3/24   Milan–San Remo, 89th

2002   *Team: Mercatone Uno*

All the allegations and court cases—another "sporting fraud" charge had been leveled against him, this time for his high hematocrit reading at the 1999 Giro—heightened The Pirate's depression and continued to affect his racing. He started the 2002 Giro but suffered like a no-hoper. He pulled out rather than live through more humiliation. As a result of the 2001 Giro drug raid, the Italian cycling federation suspended Pantani for 10 months, starting June 17. On appeal, the international sports tribunal cut the suspension by two months.

Results:
3/23   Milan–San Remo, 76th

2003 *Team: Mercatone Uno*

Despite his life's having fallen apart, Pantani began training again in the winter of 2002–2003, first in Greece, then in Spain. He split with his girlfriend, moved out of his mansion, and returned to the basics. He eventually put together a new team with the help of his first *directeur sportif* Davide Boifava—who believed that his man could still come back at age 33 to the top level.

Pantani's appearance at the Coppi & Bartali event in April was his first race in 11 months. On the final day, he took second place and placed tenth overall. While he was completing his best race since the 2000 Tour, Pantani was summoned to appear in a Trento court to open a hearing on the sporting fraud charge that followed the 1999 Giro blood test. Then he competed and completed his final Giro, having his best stage performance, fifth, on the mountaintop finish at Zoncolan. The final stage, a flat 33-kilometer time trial in Milan on June 1, was the last race of Marco Pantani's life.

Results:
3/26–30   Settimana Coppi & Bartali, 10th
5/10–6/1 Giro d'Italia, 14th
7/7–11   Tour of the Basque Country, 49th

OTHER FEATS

- Pantani wore the pink leader's jersey (*maglia rosa*) for 14 days during the 1998 and 1999 editions of the Giro d'Italia.
- Pantani wore the yellow leader's jersey (*maillot jaune*) for six days during the 1998 Tour de France.
- Pantani won the Best Climber award at the 1998 Giro.
- Pantani was the seventh rider to win the Giro and Tour in the same year (1998). The others to perform the feat were:

  Miguel Induráin (1992 and 1993)

  Stephen Roche (1987)

  Bernard Hinault (1982 and 1985)

  Eddy Merckx (1970, 1972, and 1974)

  Jacques Anquetil (1964)

  Fausto Coppi (1949 and 1952)

INDEX

PIER BERGONZI, the chief sportswriter of the Italian newspaper *La Gazzetta dello Sport*, was a confidant of Marco Pantani throughout the Italian cyclist's career. He lives in Milan, Italy.

GUILLAUME PRÉBOIS, a freelance writer for the French cycling monthly *Vélo Magazine*, is also a contributor to newspapers in France, Belgium and Switzerland. He lives in Paris and Milan.

JOHN WILCOCKSON, the editorial director of *VeloNews*, has been writing about the sport of cycling since 1968. He lives in Boulder, Colorado.